To "Buck"

A great administ[rator]

boss and a good friend.

Thanks

Roy R[ubin]

ATTACKING
BASKETBALL'S
PRESSURE
DEFENSES

ATTACKING

Prentice-Hall, Inc.

BASKETBALL'S PRESSURE DEFENSES

Roy Rubin

Englewood Cliffs, N. J.

ATTACKING BASKETBALL'S PRESSURE DEFENSES

Roy Rubin

© 1966, BY

PRENTICE-HALL, INC.

Englewood Cliffs, N.J.

LIBRARY OF CONGRESS
CATALOG CARD NUMBER: 66-19889

PRINTED IN THE UNITED STATES OF AMERICA

05025—BC

DEDICATION

To all those wonderful kids at
Christopher Columbus High School
and Long Island University who gave
so fully of themselves, who were
champions in victory and defeat, and
who proved that coaching can be the
most satisfying and most inspiring
profession in the world.

THE AGE
OF
PRESSURE
DEFENSE

ABOUT TEN TO TWENTY TIMES A YEAR EVERY BASKETBALL COACH becomes a candidate for the little man in the white coat. It can happen any time between the opening tap to a few minutes before the closing horn. The game may be going along in good fashion when, surprise! the opponents will suddenly uncork a pressure defense, and the panic will be on.

No matter what kind of personnel you have or how well you have coached your team, a pressure defense is bound to cause uncertainty and anxiety. It is a blight to a young team, a headache to an experienced team, and a pain in the brain to the coach. Nothing can turn a game around faster.

Pressure has become the name of the game. It's unquestionably the dominant force in modern basketball. Every coach worth his salt is using some form of it. What makes it so poisonously effective is its infinite variety. It can be thrown at you from a man-to-man or a zone alignment. It can be employed full-court, three-quarter-court, or half-court. It can be used with the big men or the small men as chasers. And it can be cleverly combined with the straight man-to-man or zone defense.

As long as it has mobility, the pressure defense can prove an equalizer against taller or even more talented opponents. Against slow, cumbersome, poorly organized, or inexperienced clubs, it spells murder. Nobody on offense likes to take on an opponent who is constantly swarming over him and stabbing at the ball. And even a good team can be disorganized by a defense that never lets it rest, that keeps coming at it from different directions. The best laid plans of any coach can go awry under this leeching, constant harassment.

Take UCLA in the 1964 and 1965 NCAA championships, for example. In both instances the Bruins used a full-court press to break down and destroy taller opponents. They kept applying relentless pressure from end line to mid-court until their opponents broke and started throwing the ball into their hands.

On the East coast in recent years, a small but extremely mobile St. Joseph's College team has been wearing out their opponents with an astonishing assortment of pressing defenses that challenges nearly every pass and move—double-teaming and triple-teaming the ball-handlers while still retaining court balance.

On the high school court this harassing form of defense has proved more effective. Since our schoolboys haven't the poise or experience of their college brothers, they are much more vulnerable to pressure.

The problem is obvious: Every basketball coach must learn how to handle pressure. He must study it, learn it, and discover how others are attacking it, so that he can select the method or methods most suitable to his personnel. He must then devise a sound teaching program of fundamentals, drills, and scrimmage that will inculcate the essentials simply, fully, and progressively.

Whenever I read a basketball text, I always ask myself, "Can this (or that) be used with my team?" With this in mind I'd like to present a volume of "thises" and "thats" that can be applied on every level of competition—a complete picture of a practical, progressive, and time-tested system of attacking all forms of pressure defense. It will include:

1. A basic philosophy of pressure attack.
2. Special drills and conditioning methods for the pressure attack.
3. A precise way to *teach* the individual, two-man, three-man, four-man, and five-man moves.
4. The actual mounting of the team attack against the specific forms of pressure defense.

Note that every facet of this approach is aimed at only one target —the defeat of the pressure defense. It stands to reason the more you know about it, the better equipped you will be to handle it. Where you fully prepare your boys to cope with it, they will lose only to superior teams, and not because they were unprepared either physically or mentally.

CONTENTS

Chapter 6

Chapter 7

Chapter 8

Chapter 8

CONDITIONING AND SPECIAL DRILLS VERSUS PRESSURE DEFENSES (Continued)

Chapter 9

ORGANIZATION FOR PRACTICE SCRIMMAGES **177**

Chapter 10

SYSTEMATIZED SCOUTING **185**

Chapter 10

SYSTEMATIZED SCOUTING (Continued)

ATTACKING BASKETBALL'S PRESSURE DEFENSES

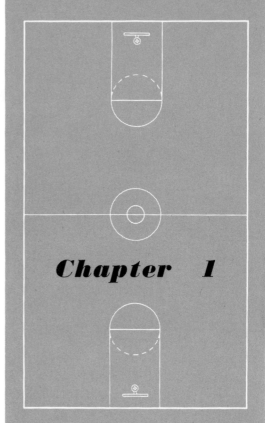

Chapter   1

SPECIAL
FUNDAMENTALS
VERSUS
PRESSURE
DEFENSES

MANY COACHES ARE INCLINED TO OVER-
look or neglect the basic fundamentals, particularly with veteran teams.
They feel that the players remember
basic skills from season to season, that
all of it is habitual.

Unfortunately, this isn't true. Even
the outstanding performers tend to
forget essential details and shy away
from the difficult job of learning. For
this reason the fundamentals of every
skill should be taught or re-taught at
the beginning of *every* season.

The degree of repetition depends

upon the experience of your squad and how much you feel they need. In any case the review of the fundamentals is a must. A thorough review will not only improve skills but will impress the boys with the importance you attach to them. Always remember that the boys will automatically follow your lead. If you skim over the fundamentals, so will they. It's only the exceptional boy who'll work without being told.

Since this book deals with pressure attack, I'd like to concentrate on the fundamentals that are particularly important against pressure defenses.

The Basic Passes

The passes we use most against pressure defense are the overhead, the bounce, and the baseball. Almost every time the defense double-teams a ball-handler, it is trying to force him into a wild pass or a violation. The trapped player will find it almost impossible to throw such passes as the chest, underhand, lob, or hand-off. This doesn't mean that we ignore these passes. It does mean that we concentrate on the others whenever we're practicing and thinking of pressure defenses.

There's nothing more frustrating to the defense than a team that can pass and handle the ball. Whenever the ball is passed so that the receiver can quickly dribble, pass, or shoot it, the pressure defense will be in trouble. They'll find it difficult to harass an opponent who can pass over, under, or around their hands.

Passing Pointers

We insist upon certain rules against pressure—rules that we hope will become habits. We don't want anyone stopping in the middle of a play and saying, "The coach told me to hold my fingers this way." Nor do we want a boy who has just thrown the ball away tell us, "Coach, you instructed me to only use the overhead pass whenever I'm trapped."

Following are some of the rules we emphasize:

1. *Don't turn your back on the basket* when you're attacked. It then becomes impossible to make the pass you want. You'll be throwing a protective pass rather than penetrating the defense. There'll be

times when you'll have to turn your back, but this shouldn't become a regular thing.

2. *Force the defense to attack you.* Bait them into committing themselves by taking the ball to a particular area of the court.

3. *Spread the pressure defense* so that the chasers will have a lot of additional territory to cover.

4. *Be ready to receive a pass at any time,* and be alert to assist a trapped teammate.

5. *Move toward the ball,* particularly when a teammate needs help; this will facilitate his pass.

6. *Use the entire width of the court;* don't let the defense trap you into dribbling off to a side or corner.

7. *Anticipate the defensive attack;* this should be uppermost in mind against pressure defenses.

8. *"Swallow the ball"* rather than throw it away. Whenever you're tied up, avoid the blind desperation pass or the steal. Put the ball against your stomach so that at worst you'll get a jump ball.

Pressure will affect all ballplayers, even the pros. How badly you're hurt by it will depend on how well and how consistently you can handle it at various stages of the game.

Before setting up the boys in any specific attacking pattern, we go over the basics of the essential passes.

Mechanics of the Overhead Pass

We start with medicine balls, pairing off two boys to a ball, to assure hard and continuous work. The medicine ball becomes heavy after about five minutes, and we then switch to a basketball. The boys enjoy the switch, being amused by the difference in weight and the ease with which they can now pass.

We tell them to hold the ball straight up in the air, avoiding any bend in the elbows. We want to make them as tall as possible. We look for a boy who is bending his elbows, and point out how this makes him anywhere from six to twelve inches smaller.

One of the cardinal rules of passing is fingertip control. This certainly should be taught. Sometimes, however, you'll get a boy who uses a great deal of palm but still manages to pass and shoot well. It's wise to leave this boy alone.

Either leg may be extended toward the target, and the ball should

Photo 2

Photo 1

Photo 3

be thrown on a straight line with no loops. The pass should be aimed high enough to force the receiver to reach for it.

The coach and his assistant should appraise each basic of the pass, and immediately correct any error. The pause for correction is also helpful in that it gives everyone a breather.

The pass should be demonstrated by two boys who understand what you want. Whenever you find two boys who are passing incorrectly, direct the squad's attention to them to illustrate the wrong way. This should be done, of course, with a minimum of embarrassment.

Whenever you switch from the medicine ball to the regular ball, you'll often find the boys throwing it over each other's head. Sometimes this is due simply to the weight differential. Other times it will be due to mechanical errors. If the boys are making some basic mistake, they should be stopped for re-instruction before continuing with the drill.

Mechanics of the Bounce Pass

One of the basic fundamentals of pressure defense is to close in with the hands held high. The defensive hands occupy a lot of court

Photos 1-5. OVERHEAD JUMP PASS: This is a particularly effective pass for double-team situations. Whenever the player is being harassed in a way that prevents him from firing a direct pass to a teammate, he can extend the ball overhead, leap into the air, and whip it with a strong wrist action. Note how both arms are completely extended on the jump, and how the ball is controlled with the fingers rather than the palms.

Photo 5

Photo 4

space and often prevent the ball-handler from seeing his target. That's why coaches are always screaming "Hands up!" or griping about the difficulty of getting kids to play defense with their hands up.

It's easy to understand why the bounce pass is so essential against a pressure defense. The guards almost always have their hands up, and it's definitely easier to go under rather than over them.

The fundamentals of the bounce pass are similar in some ways to those of the other passes. First we expect our boys to control the ball with their fingertips rather than palms. We start with the conventional two-hand bounce pass.

Our boys pair up, facing each other about six to eight feet apart. The passer assumes a crouch in which his body almost forms the letter "C." He holds the ball with his fingertips and steps toward his target with either foot, delivering the ball with a slight reverse spin.

Since we don't want the ball to bounce too high, we insist that it be delivered no higher than the receiver's knee. We encourage the passer to hit the floor more than halfway to his target so that the ball won't bounce too high before reaching the target.

The receiver is supposed to catch the ball with the fingertips much in the manner of a shortstop. He must move toward the ball with hands outstretched and return the ball after catching it properly.

We again demonstrate both the correct and incorrect forms.

After teaching the two-hand bounce pass, we move to the one-hand pass. The fundamentals are basically the same, except that the boys exhibit a tendency to curve the ball and thus make it harder to receive. Emphasis on the proper release action will eliminate curves. The ball must be released with a straight wrist. If the boy continues to pitch curves, he should receive some private instruction.

The players should learn to bounce-pass with either hand, two hands, sidearm, and through a guard's legs (which sometimes is necessary in a game).

This can be a difficult pass to receive if (1) too much spin is put on the ball, (2) it's thrown too low to a player cutting for the hoop, or (3) it's thrown behind the cutter.

A properly delivered bounce pass is an excellent weapon because most guards play with their hands up and usually don't expect the ball to be passed under them.

Mechanics of the Baseball Pass

The baseball pass is most often used to launch the fast break. It can be thrown long or short as well as very fast, and thus offers an extremely effective tool with which to beat the defense down the floor and prevent it from setting up. Though it can be a difficult pass for young boys with small hands, anyone can master it with practice.

We again start with a medicine ball, with the boys paired off some six to eight feet apart. The passer grips the ball with both hands, one on either side, with the throwing hand usually a little higher on the ball; the other hand is used for balance and control.

The ball is cocked up near the ear to prevent a long windup and to aid a quick release. (Don't worry if your boys complain that it's uncomfortable to hold a medicine ball in two hands up near the ear.) To achieve full power on the throw the player must extend the leg opposite the throwing arm and get his shoulder behind the throw. He should aim for his teammate's shoulders.

The receiver should take the ball on the run without bending or breaking stride. (With a medicine ball this throw requires a great deal of strength, but it affords excellent practice.) The receiver must catch the ball with his fingertips without staggering too much, then immediately put it to his ear, step out, and throw it right back.

This should be repeated without hesitation to develop the habit of getting rid of the ball quickly. The boys should alternate throwing arms, as they'll often be called upon to throw the ball from different positions and angles.

After five good minutes with the heavy ball, you should switch to the basketball. Again the boys will feel as though they can throw the ball ten miles, and may become careless. Whenever they start throwing the ball all over the gym, the coach must step in, make corrections, have player demonstrations, and then continue practice.

The Follow-Through

As you may have noticed, so far I've omitted any reference to the follow-through. I've done this intentionally, saving it for special emphasis.

The follow-through is the final and most important step in passing. The ball won't go toward its target unless the throwing hand "points the way." If the hand goes up or down at the end of the pass, the ball will have a tendency to fly off-line. The hand must be extended directly at the target. During the practice with the medicine ball, the follow-through should be exaggerated.

On the overhead pass we make our boys lock their thumbs after the release to prevent them from lapsing into the habit of pulling their arms apart (away from the target). We observe the same procedure on any other two-hand pass that we may use. The idea is to accustom the boys to keep their arms close together and as close to the body as possible.

For the baseball pass we want them to extend their arm toward the target with the fingers completely extended.

These fundamental drills should be done every day with medicine balls until the players have reaped full value from the heavy ball with respect to strength and technique. We generally give up the medicine ball after a week. With high school boys, especially young ones, it may be wise to use them for a longer period of time.

Photo 1   **Photo 2**

Photos 1-6. BASEBALL PASS (RIGHT AND LEFT): The value of an ambidextrous rebounder is graphically illustrated in these sequences. When rebounding on the left side of the board, the player should be able to pitch out with his right hand. On the right side, he should be able to pitch with his left hand. Note how the player spread-eagles on the rebound and how he quickly turns up-court. The ball is not brought all the way down. To assure a quick get-away, the player keeps the ball around the ear and pitches without any extravagant cocking action. He gets the zip from a powerful forearm and wrist action. The overhand movement and straight wrist prevent curves.

Photo 4

Photo 3

Photo 5

Photo 6

11

Photo 1

Photo 2

BASEBALL PASS
(RIGHT AND LEFT)
(continued)

Photo 4

Photo 3

Photo 5

Photo 6

Shooting Fundamentals Versus Pressure Defenses

Most teams get two distinctly different types of shots against a pressure defense. One is the rushed and hurried shot, which you don't really want, and the other is the wide-open shot.

The passing skills previously covered play an important role in getting the type of shot you want. The good pass will enable you to shoot, dribble, or pass to greatest advantage.

Since you sometimes get wide-open shots, have every boy practice from the areas that you expect to put them during games. This is a must that should be done during the shooting part of practice every day. It's strange, but true, that it's sometimes more difficult for a boy to shoot with nobody on him than it is when he's completely covered. It seems that the more time he has to make up his mind, the more uncertain he often becomes.

The shots under pressure can be practiced in various ways. Perhaps the simplest way is for the shooter to have a partner run at him during practice. Before delving into any other ways of teaching shooting under pressure, I'd like to analyze the shots that we've found most effective against pressure defenses. These are, in order, the jump shot (standing still or on the move) and the driving layup.

Of course there are a great many other shots that you'll get from time to time, like the hook, set, one-hand push, etc., but the jumper and the driving layup remain the primary weapons against zone presses. We concentrate on these two shots in all of our work against such defenses.

Mechanics of the Jump Shot

The jump shot is extremely flexible. Players can shoot it standing still or moving, facing the basket or with their backs to the basket, and from practically any angle—falling away or going toward the basket. This has become the hardest shot to defense in the history of the game.

In teaching the jump shot, we have the boy bring his feet close together to gather for the jump. The average boy will require a little momentum or power if he's standing still. He can get this power by faking with one foot and then bringing it quickly back close to the other, keeping his knees bent and most of his weight on the balls of his feet.

He's now ready to spring. We want him to get up as high as he can and hang in the air while lining up his shot. The better jumpers can hang a little longer and with better body balance, making it even tougher on the defender. Some of them (Elgin Baylor is the classic example) can even throw a fake while in the air.

The ball is still held in both hands while the boy is leaping. The shooting hand is automatically placed on the side and under the ball, so that the ball seems to be resting on the palm, as on a cup or a tee. The non-shooting hand is placed on the side toward the front of the ball, and is used strictly as a balancer.

At the top of the jump, the balance hand is removed and the shooter delivers the ball, the shooting arm straightening out so that the arm and fingers are fully extended toward the target.

The player must shoot at the peak of his leap or, sometimes, on the way down, but *never* on the way up, as his balance and momentum at that time forbid accuracy.

Mechanics of the Driving Layup

The layup appears to be the easiest shot in the game. Yet how many times have you seen good ballplayers blow the shot under pressure? This is a "must score" shot, particularly against pressure defenses that play everyone tight and tough. This sort of defense opens the door to those fat three-point plays.

Being the most elementary shot in the game, the layup requires no detailed analysis in a book of this nature. Suffice it to say that the right-hander should shoot off the left foot and the left-hander off the right foot.

The leap should be a maximum effort, as the closer you get to the basket the shorter and the easier the shot. The ball should be carried up with both hands. Upon the release the non-shooting hand should be thrust out for protection against anyone trying to block the shot. I don't want my players to put any spin on the ball. I want them to lay the ball flatly and gently against the board about a foot above the rim.

We don't care whether the boy holds his shooting hand under or behind the ball. We allow him to shoot it either way, whichever is

Photo 3

Photo 2

Photos 1-6. JUMP SHOT: The jumper is the money shot against pressure defenses. Many players have their own individual style; but as long as it's effective, the coach shouldn't tamper with it. As you may observe in these sequences, the first player shoots in the classic overhead fashion, while the other brings the ball a bit out to the side. The form in both cases is exemplary. The ball is brought up

Photo 1

16

Photo 4

Photo 5

Photo 6

Jump Shot (cont.)

with both hands, the left serving as a balancer and the right being directly under the ball. The player bends slightly at the knees and goes straight up, folding the shooting forearm back. He hangs for a moment, releases the balancing hand, and shoots with an extension of the forearm. The ball comes off the fingertips, with the hand following through in superlative fashion.

17

Photo 1

Photo 3

Photo 2

Jump Shot (style two)

18

Photo 4

Photo 6

Photo 5

19

Photo 1   Photo 2

Photos 1-6. DRIVING LAY-UP: This is the sort of shot that every player must master, as nobody can afford to blow such opportunities against the pressure or any other defense. Along with the jumper, it's the bread-and-butter shot of basketball. The shooting form here is of the picture variety. The player takes a gorgeous long last step and launches into the air, bringing the ball up with both hands. He lets his momentum carry him into the basket, during which he removes his balancing (left) hand and fully extends his shooting arm. Although just 6-1 he goes right up to the rim and lays the ball gently over it.

Photo 4

Photo 3

Photo 5   Photo 6

21

Photo 1

Photo 2

Photo 3

Photos 1-8. MODIFIED HOOK: The pivot man glides into the lane with a low, controlled dribble, then goes up as high as he can. He hangs for a moment, then releases the ball softly off the fingertips with a nice wrist action. Note how he keeps his eye on the hoop and how he leans in while shooting.

Photo 4

Demonstrated by Albie Grant, Long Island University

Photo 5

Photo 6

Photo 7

Photo 8

Photos 1-8. DIP SHOT: The player maneuvers to a spot in front of the hoop, then launches into outer space. At the peak of his jump, with his body under perfect control, he extends his arm and dips the ball just over the rim with a neat forearm action.

| Photo 1 | Photo 2 | Photo 3 | Photo 4 |

Photo 5   Photo 6   Photo 7   Photo 8

Demonstrated by Albie Grant, Long Island University

Photo 1   **Photo 2**

Photos 1-8. REVERSE MOVE: Grant pivots left as if to move into the lane. As his man leans that way, Grant drives inside him for the lay-up. Note that he starts with a small left step—this is a travel. Having established the left as the pivot foot, he should have driven directly off it.

Photo 4

Photo 3

Photo 5   Photo 6   Photo 7   Photo 8

Demonstrated by Albie Grant, Long Island University

more comfortable and easier for him, unless he is having trouble with his layup—then we'll recommend one style or the other.

In our practice drills we insist that the boys shoot right-handed on the right side of the basket and left-handed on the left side. We try to develop ambidexterity to make the boy feel equally at home with both hands. During the game, however, there are no restrictions. The boy can shoot with the hand that feels best for him. What's best for him is usually best for the team.

The old theory that every boy should shoot the same way is passé. The modern kid is too individualistic and too talented to be restricted in this fashion. I'm more interested in having the boys take good percentage shots than in working for the picture jump shot or layup. Against pressure defenses you have other things to worry about than perfect-looking shots.

Shooting Drills

The jump and layup shots are practiced in various ways every day throughout the entire practice season.

Fig. 1-1: We set up a shooting line along the side of the midcourt line and a defensive line about three yards back and more toward the middle of the court. The offensive players dribble in hard for the layup, while the defensive men try to block the shot cleanly without fouling or goaltending. This gives the layup man good practice in shooting against a man who's breathing down his neck.

Fig. 1-2: The jump shot is practiced from a two-man moving situation. The guard passes to a forward, goes behind, gets the ball back, and shoots his jumper.

Fig. 1-3: The forward feeds the center and cuts off him for his jump shot.

Fig. 1-4: The center is fed from the side and shoots turn-around jumpers from the pivot, each man practicing his own type of shot.

Fig. 1-5: We place three balloon-type dummies across the three-second area—one on each buffer line and the third just inside the foul line. Our shooting lines go one at a time. Each boy goes as hard as he can toward the dummy, then pulls up or maneuvers his body around the dummy for the jumper. The lines are rotated right to left to give each boy an opportunity to shoot from the three different areas of the court.

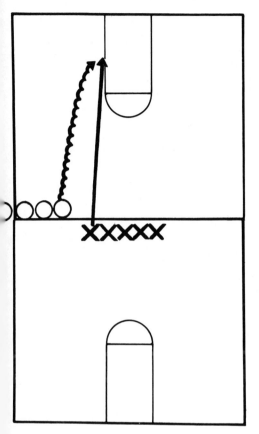

Figure 1-1. Pressure Layup Drill

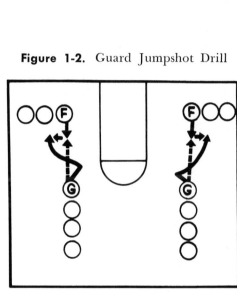

Figure 1-2. Guard Jumpshot Drill

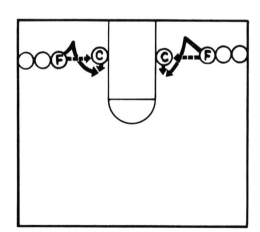

Figure 1-3. Forward Jump Shot Drill

29

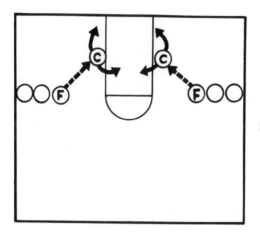

Figure 1-4. Center Jump Shot Drill

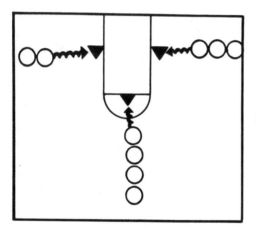

Figure 1-5. Pressure Jump Shot Drill

This has always been one of our key drills for perfecting the jump shot against pressure, and it also helps the boys learn to avoid charging into stationary defensive players. It's important to let the team know the purpose of all the fundamentals and drills that you work on.

Mechanics of Dribbling

To beat pressing defenses, your players must know how to dribble, when to dribble, when not to dribble, who should dribble, and how to coordinate their dribbling skills with their passing and shooting.

As a prime weapon against pressure, the dribble should be a purposeful move that ends up in a scoring situation.

Good dribbling is predicated upon a sure touch with the ball. Some boys are naturally endowed with extra long fingers and hands and an easy flexible wrist movement. But even they require practice to become outstanding dribblers.

The good dribbler moves from a crouch with the knees slightly bent, the head up, and the ball off to the side of the body. The ball is controlled with the fingertips, with the power stemming from the wrist movement. The ball must strike the floor hard enough to bounce back to an even level; but not so hard that it booms back too fast to be controlled.

The ball must also be protected by the body. The dribbler should practice dribbling sideways, back and forth, and up and down the court. He should also practice going backwards, and changing hands on every bounce to develop proficiency with both hands.

The dribbler can keep the ball away from his guard by bouncing it to the side or sometimes almost behind him. The idea is to prevent the guard from reaching the ball without hitting the dribbler's body. The protection of the ball is always enhanced by dribbling with the hand away from the defensive player. This is a must in teaching the fundamentals.

The basics, then, consist of:

1. Fingertip control.
2. Protection of the ball.
3. Keeping the head up (to see what's going on around you).
4. Keeping the body low.
5. Using the hand away from the defensive man.
6. Properly bouncing the ball off the floor (for control).
7. Mastery of both hands.

There are two types of dribbles for the advanced player—the high dribble and the low dribble. The high dribble is used for speed during a break-away when you want fewer and longer bounces. The low dribble is employed for maneuverability by the good backcourt man, generally for dribbling around a defender.

There's also a "drag dribble" that's used by pivot men. With their back to the basket, they move to either side (maneuvering into position for a shot, particularly the hook or jumper), while dragging the ball with them. To avoid being called for traveling, they must bounce the ball once or twice.

The dribbling drills should be designed in the form of competition (races) to prevent boredom.

The amount of dribbling you do against pressure defenses should depend upon the location of your break-away and the set-up of the defense.

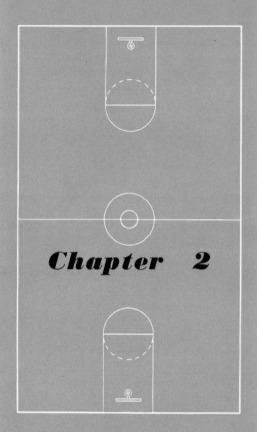

Chapter 2

ORGANIZING THE ATTACK AGAINST PRESSURE DEFENSE

AT LONG ISLAND UNIVERSITY, WE ALWAYS expect the worst. We expect to be hit with some type of pressure defense in every ball game. We therefore work long, hard, and systematically. We want our players to know certain principles and to learn them through daily practice. Following are some of the essentials that we try to "sell" to our players:

1. We must practice against pressure defenses daily, as we're sure to meet some type of pressure in every ball game.

2. We must practice under game conditions whenever possible. The use of the clock, officials, and the setting up of game situations are extremely helpful in getting the players to understand what they're expected to do in varying situations.

3. Regardless of how we eventually break the pressure, we want to *go immediately to the basket;* we're not satisfied with merely getting the ball over the mid-court line.

4. We must look for the three-on-two or any odd-man situation and make sure to get the good shot at the end of it.

5. After beating the defensive team down the floor, we don't want the pressure to reform easily. That means that no one player should "sit" on the ball. We want to *keep the ball moving.*

6. We want to *move the ball forward,* not laterally. Lateral movement is permissible only in emergency situations.

7. We want to *limit our dribbling* against a pressure defense. The ball can move faster than a dribbler, and zone presses want you to dribble so that they can double-team you.

8. We always must have a *series of post men* ready to receive a pass from any trapped teammates.

9. The post men must give *good targets.* They must be seen by the trapped players and must attempt to clear themselves from any defensive players who are overplaying them.

The post men don't necessarily have to be big men. We want players who are agile enough to handle the ball properly after receiving it and being attacked.

With this sort of program, the players must be sold on what you're trying to do on a team basis. They must understand your thinking on handling pressure and why you have selected your particular techniques. If they don't know what you're trying to do and why, they'll have a much more difficult time learning and implementing your theories.

The Basic Attacking Weapon

Perhaps the first thing to understand about pressure is that it's a gambling defense. The defense is geared to make you rush, throw the ball away, and generally unhinge your offense. You must score easy baskets against it or you and your players will be in for a long evening. The trick lies in discouraging the pressure with proper ball-handling and easy shots.

That's why I believe that every offense should be prepared to fast break against it, regardless of whether you believe in the control type of game or a mixture of possession and fast break. The pressure defense will force your boys to go to the basket, and they had better be prepared to go properly.

A good example of this was St. John's University against Boston College in the 1965 NIT. Coach Joe Lapchick was hardly a staunch protagonist of the fast break. He liked to play a sound, simple, and hard-nosed brand of possession basketball. But when Boston College pressed, then zone pressed, they forced St. John's to run more than they desired.

Though Coach Lapchick's pre-game plan was to hold the ball and not run with B.C., the Redmen handled the pressure so well that night that they went over 100 points. The moral is that they were ready when forced into a running game. They took the right opportunities and hit their shots.

Organization of Progression Drills

In organizing our attack against pressure defenses, we break down our patterns into "progression" drills, starting with groups of two and then working into three-man, four-man, and finally five-man attacks. As the drills progress from two men to five, a picture of the overall attack begins to emerge, enabling the boys to grasp what we're trying to accomplish.

Starting with small groups also enables us to give special attention to those who may need it, and to give the boys more work on specific situations. The progressive drills are particularly helpful to coaches with such problems as late classes and small squads, where an absentee or an injury could seriously hamper the practice session. The two, three, four, and five-man offensive maneuvers give the coach a variety of practice drills for special purposes and situations.

If you wish to work with only a few boys, you can. If you want to give extra work to a few, you can. The boys can also work on their own in small groups. They don't have to look for nine teammates.

By the time we begin actual work on our pressure attack, we

assume that our boys are in shape, thanks to all of our early-season drills (which will be described later on).

The Two-Man Attack

We start with a two-man attack against a two-man pressure defense, pairing off the boys according to ability. That is, we try to match speed with speed and size with size.

As soon as the drill is mastered, we mix up sizes and speeds so that the boys can get used to attacking any unusual setup. The reason for this is that all teams play their pressure defenses a little differently. Some will play their biggest boys all over the court in the hope that your guards won't be able to see over them or pass over them with any degree of accuracy. Other teams will use their quick little men as chasers and gamble for steals, knowing that they still have defense at the other end of the court.

Before starting the drills, we inform the players either through a short talk or a blackboard demonstration of exactly what we're trying to do, what we want to accomplish as a team, and what we expect of each individual. Each player must know his role in the attack.

If you get a boy who feels he can't excel whenever he's told precisely what to do and thus can't use his own ingenuity, you must give him special work. He must be taught to understand that basketball is a team game and that he'll have all types of opportunities to prove his individuality in the framework of the team effort. In fact the drills and attacks are primarily designed to protect the boy from losing his individuality. But if he doesn't know where to go and what the other team is doing, he won't have the opportunity to display his individual talent.

Some boys require a bigger selling job than others. Generally this conflict arises with talented boys. The boys who can't do anything individually won't give you any problem; they'll be happy to serve as robots. We don't want robots, but we must be prepared to coach all types of boys and find a place for them on offense and defense.

As shown in FIG. 2-1, the boys are paired off in two lines under one of the baskets. One boy takes the ball out of bounds while the other is being pressed and overplayed by his defensive man. The easiest move for the inside man is to fake coming to the ball, then break down the court all the way. Unfortunately, this opportunity

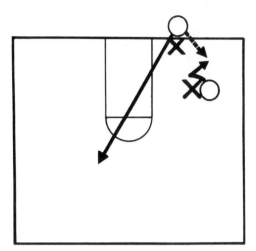

Figure 2-1. Two-Man Pressure
Attack

doesn't occur too often because there are other defensive men down the court who can intercept the long "touchdown pass."

We try to encourage the boys to get the ball in safely from out of bounds. To do this the inside man must maneuver his guard with fakes and feints and come to the ball. If he doesn't, the outside man will commit a five-second violation. Every time we have a five-second violation in practice, we penalize the would-be receiver.

The man guarding the out-of-bounds passer plays him right along the end line, jumping up and down and otherwise harassing the thrower without committing a violation. We want him to observe the rules; we don't want him to step or place his hands or body across the line in bothering the passer. We call this our "Don't Let Him Die" drill.

Once the ball is passed in from out of bounds, we have the thrower *go away* from the receiver, letting the latter bring the ball down alone in a one-on-one situation. This is a good practice against opponents who apply only one-on-one pressure. If you have a good dribbler, you should attempt to free him so that he can bring the ball down for you.

This drill enables everyone on the squad to learn how to dribble against a man his size, and it gives you an opportunity to add variety to your attack. Sometimes you can bring your big man back to move the ball up the floor, particularly if he's playing against a big man who is not as agile as he and cannot press him easily.

When the boys reach the offensive end of the floor, they continue to play according to their specific positions. If we have guards playing guards, they work from the guard area of the court on two-man guard plays. If we have a combination of a guard and a forward, they work our two-man plays from these areas. The same holds true with a guard-center combination, the center playing either the high post or a deep pivot position.

We always get the guards to work with forwards or centers. We discourage four forwards going at once. We want them to get practice on the offensive end of the court, since they'll be playing the same general areas in the game. The drill, incidentally, is also excellent for developing your defensive skills.

Variation of Two-Man Attack

Fig. 2-2 shows a variation of the two-man drill—the two defensive players double-team the receiver, leaving the out-of-bounds man completely alone; their objective is to prevent the pass from coming in. The defense must be quick and sure, as the passer will be free if he does get the pass in. This applies additional pressure on the receiver, and he must learn to move, fake, and feint to prevent his teammate from committing a five-second violation.

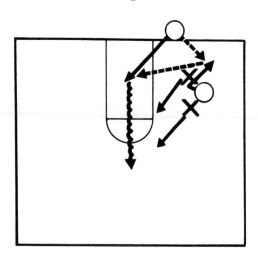

Figure 2-2. Variation of Two-Man Attack

The outside thrower must immediately cut away from the receiver and be ready to get a quick, short return pass and go directly downcourt to the basket as hard as he can. The defense must pursue and make an attempt to catch and stop the man from making the easy basket.

In both drills, after a good shot has been taken, we reverse the positions and have the boys come back down the court, the defensive team now becoming the offensive team and vice-versa.

The Three-Man Attack

Once distinct progress has been made in our two-man drill, we progress to three.

The boys like the drill better, as it gives them more security on the floor. It becomes a little more difficult for the offense to get away, and a boy's glaring mistakes cannot be seen as readily with the extra two men on the court. The less experienced and less talented players always live in fear of the glaring error. Ergo the cry, "The coach has no confidence in me; one mistake and I'm out."

FIG. 2-3. We start by forming three lines—as always, the guards going with the forwards and centers. While we don't discourage anyone from dribbling, we want them to get used to the positions they'll be playing in the games and to get them organized against pressure.

One man takes the ball out of bounds. Though we don't want a

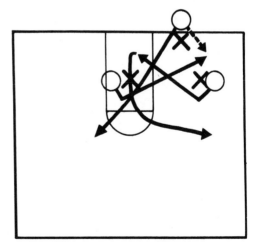

Figure 2-3. Three-Man Pressure Attack

poor ball-handler taking the ball out of bounds in game situations, all should work at it in the drills. The problem in most cases is that the best ball-handler is also your best dribbler and passer. The coach thus has a decision to make as to who should handle the ball and how to set up.

We have several variations. Our first is primarily for guards. As shown in FIG. 2-3, we'll have two men criss-cross so as to confuse the defensive men and cause a poor switch. The defenders must overplay their men completely in order to make the receivers move and fake correctly to receive the ball.

Once the ball is passed in from out-of-bounds, the thrower and the other man who didn't receive the ball always *go away* from the receiver. They look for a return pass if they're free and always look back to see whether the man is in trouble. Sometimes he'll be double or triple-teamed.

Again we penalize the receivers if they cause the outside man to commit a five-second violation. After several practice sessions, we also penalize poor passing and lost balls. We strive for perfection, even though we know we won't get 100%. This helps develop good habits and makes the players put out 100% all of the time.

When they bring the ball into the offensive half of the court, they work into the positions they'll normally be playing in the game. From there we concentrate on whatever play situations we want to develop, depending on what combinations of guards, forwards, and centers we have on the court at the time.

At the completion of a good shot, the defensive team switches with the offense. If the shot is missed, the defensive team must block out and get the rebound. If the offense gets the rebound, they continue to set up their three-man attack. If the defensive team gets the rebound, we blow the whistle. Play is stopped and they take the ball out of bounds for an assault in the opposite direction.

Variation of the Three-Man Attack

There are many variations of the three-man attack, depending on how you set up your defensive men.

We practice one particular variation which combines a zone and man-to-man pressure. This suffices until we get into our four- and five-man attacks.

In our first basic three-man attack (Fig. 2-3), all three men were under pressure as they were all being closely guarded. In this variation (Fig. 2-4) we take the guard off the outside man and place him between the two offensive receivers. This drill makes the offense really work under pressure, though it's not necessarily the best way to break up different pressure defenses (which will be explained later on).

The defensive man between the two receivers has the option of faking with his shoulders, hips, eyes, etc., to entice the outside man into passing in the direction he wants him to. As soon as the pass is made, the mid-defender becomes a double-teamer. The offense is supposed to react quickly. It must get the ball back to the free man and down the floor for an odd-man advantage shot. The defense must also react quickly and pick up the free man, pressuring him until the defender who has lost his man recovers a free man.

This drill forces the offensive team to handle the ball well in dangerous territory, where every mistake may cost them a basket. The offense must be sold on the fact that only panic will hurt them. If each man moves quickly toward the ball and knows where his teammates are going and that they'll be there to help him, the offense can destroy the pressure by scoring easy baskets.

Once the ball goes down the floor in this drill, the offensive team looks for the fast break and shot. If they don't get the good shot, they take the ball out and maneuver into a three-man attack.

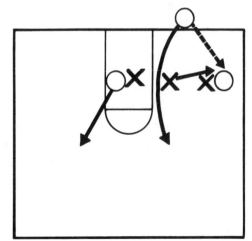

Figure 2-4. Variation of Three-Man Attack

As before, the six men play until a shot is taken, missed, and recovered by the defensive team. The defense then takes the ball out of bounds and brings the ball down the floor. Though we're not studying defense as such in this book, these drills automatically develop your defense and give you varieties to work with in a game. The stress should be on developing your defense as well as your offense in all of these drills.

The Four-Man Attack

By the time your team completes all of the two- and three-man drills, they'll have begun to understand what you're trying to teach them. The four-man attack sharpens their focus, and the picture of the overall attack begins to emerge.

The entire squad should be exposed to all of these drills, not just the first five, six, or seven men. Coaches who work only with their so-called first team, to the neglect of the remaining boys, are making a serious blunder. Every boy should be prepared properly for their role on the team, even if it will be confined to brief and infrequent appearances in the ball game. That one appearance might cost you a game if the boy was only used as a dummy in practice.

It's the coach's responsibility to see that all of the boys are learning the same fundamental principles and practicing them daily. This year's sophomores will probably be next year's regulars, so get them ready.

In the four-man attack we usually work with a combination of two guards and two forwards, or two guards, one forward and a center. We try to keep the guards on the floor at all times, as they're the men who will do most of the ball-handling, plus set up the offense, control the pace of the game, provide leadership, and set up all of the players on the floor.

We want all of the boys to get used to playing with the guards. We also vary the different combinations so that the boys will get used to playing with everyone on the squad instead of just the starting players. We expect the guards to be able to pass properly to each player on the team. They must know the abilities of the forwards, centers, and fellow guards.

We continually stress the "good pass"—a throw that the receiver can handle properly and quickly get into position to shoot, pass, or dribble. Many young boys will tend to pass the ball exactly the same way to each boy on the team. Some will be able to catch the ball, some won't. The young passer will blame the receiver for missing his pass. We make the passer understand that each teammate needs a different type of pass and that the good passer will vary his technique for each boy.

We want our guards to give us as much leadership as possible on the floor, with help from anyone who can contribute it. As shown in Fig. 2-5, Guard No. 1 takes the ball out of bounds, while the other guard (No. 2) sets up three or four yards away from the end line. The latter makes a concerted effort to free himself and come toward the ball.

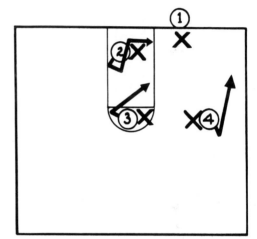

Figure 2-5. Four-Man Pressure Attack

The two forwards deploy parallel with the foul line or between the foul line and the top of the circle. One forward (No. 4) sets up near the sideline closer to the ball, while the other sets up near the foul-line area. The forwards, in order to free themselves, can either set up as post men or can take three steps upcourt, then turn quickly and fish-hook back for the pass. The forwards must come to the pass. The defense is gambling, and the forward can't stand still and wait for the ball. If he does, chances are that his defensive man will come from behind and either steal the ball or slap it away. Your boys must be sold on ball-possession and proper movement in this area of the court. Any ball loss on your end of the court will usually cost you heavily.

FIG. 2-6: If the ball is thrown into the guard, the out-of-bounds passer must *go away* from his pass in order to take his defensive man with him, while the two forwards slowly move downcourt, watching to see if the guard needs additional help.

Once the ball is brought into the offensive area, the four men set up in their natural offensive positions and work on their team patterns. Again we play until the defensive team recovers the rebound from either a missed shot or a scored basket. The four-man teams then reverse assignments and come back down the floor.

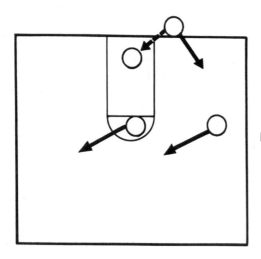

Figure 2-6. Pass-In and Go-Away

In our first four-man drill (FIG. 2-5), we play our defensive men right on top of the offensive players and have them try to make the offense commit a mistake in getting the ball in from out of bounds. We then vary the defensive set-up to resemble different types of zone pressures (FIGS. 2-7, 8).

The emphasis is always on knowing where to go and preventing the loss of the ball. All of your players must be prepared for the pressure. You don't want your inexperienced boys running away from the ball. This sometimes leads to three or four quick steals by the defense, which can turn a game around.

Pressure even upsets experienced players. That's why we feel it's

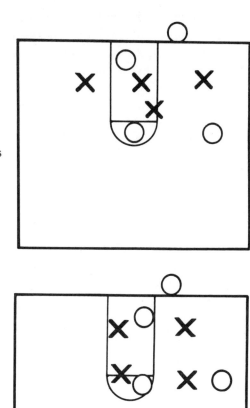

Figure 2-7. Start of 3-1-1 Press

Figure 2-8. The 2-2 Zone Press

important to play against it daily. Practicing this way is invaluable in that it accustoms the boys to someone hanging on their neck all the time. It also helps your defensive outlook. We constantly ask our boys, "What kind of a defensive player do you want to guard you?" They invariably answer, "One who doesn't bother you all the time."

Variations of the Four-Man Attack

In our first variation we set the defense up into the beginning of a 3-1-1 zone press (FIG. 2-7).

We allow the ball to come into the guard and then double-team him immediately. If he gets the ball back to the forward properly and quickly, the other forward will start to break for the basket, and we should have a good odd-man situation for a fast break and shot. We're looking for the good shot on the offensive end of the court. If we cannot get the good shot, we throw the ball out and reset the offense.

In the next variation the defense is set up in a 2-2 formation (FIG. 2-8). The offense is allowed to throw the ball in, but the receiver

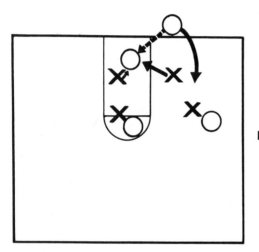

Figure 2-9. Double-Team on Guard

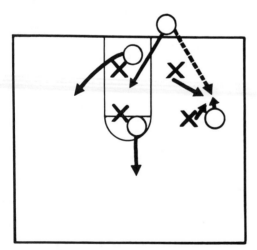

Figure 2-10. Double-Team on Forward

is immediately double-teamed. FIG. 2-9 shows the double-teaming of the guard, and FIG. 2-10 the double-teaming of the forward.

Once again the boys must get the ball into play safely, cut away from their teammate to prevent another defensive man from coming into the play, look for a return pass, and always be on the alert for the fast break and odd-man situation.

Since the defense has three or four players down at this end of the court, proper ball-handling will catch them short in the offensive end. A "rear mirror" perception is vitally important on the down-court break. Some boys, while beating their man down the floor, forget that he's chasing them, and allow him to catch up and swat the ball away from behind.

If the fast break shot doesn't materialize, the boys again go into their basic pattern of offense and play it until the defensive team recovers the ball. No matter how well the boys have been moving the ball, the stoppage of play never lets them forget that they've only been drilling. Actually, in all of our drill so far, we've been working on our attack against pressure as well as our pattern against a man-to-man defense in the offensive end of the court.

The boys are now hungry and eager to go full court. We encourage this feeling. We want them looking forward to scrimmaging full court without too many stops. It generates interest and motivates practice.

Having progressed through the two, three, and four-man drills, we're now ready to work on the five-man attack.

The Five-Man Attack

Each unit that goes up and down the floor has two guards, a center, and two forwards. We don't work them as first or second teams at this stage of practice. We want all of the boys to get the same work in the drills and to feel that progress in the drills will enhance their chances to play regularly. We don't want last year's starters to sit back and think that they have it made.

The mixture of veterans and newcomers in various combinations also gives the weaker players more incentive and develops them to the point where they'll be able to make a contribution either in the games or as good practice players who'll push the regulars in the daily practice sessions.

Fig. 2-11 shows the man-to-man pressure alignment. The offense has the two guards, or a guard and a forward, criss-cross under the basket in order to shake loose for the inbounds pass. The two bigger men, usually the center and a forward, set up parallel to the foul lines and can either fish-hook or set themselves up as post men, depending on how the defense is playing them. The out-of-bounds man thus has four optional receivers for the pass.

As before we want our receivers to get the ball within five seconds; otherwise they'll be penalized. Our penalties hinge upon the seriousness of the misdemeanor. The usual penalty consists of two laps backwards around the gym, which are taken at the end of practice, as will be explained in our practice organization later on.

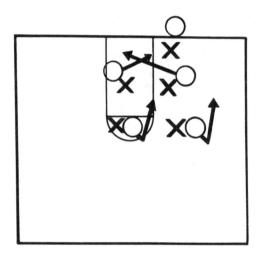

Figure 2-11. Five-Man Attack vs Pressure

Variations of the Five-Man Attack

Figs. 2-12 and 13 delineate two different defensive formations that we use to complicate the offensive team's job of getting the ball into play easily. Both formations are types of zone presses which convert into man-to-man presses whenever the offense gets the ball in and maneuvers it over the mid-court line.

Fig. 2-12 shows a 3-2 defensive formation and our loose 1-2-2 against it. We study the offensive alignment carefully as a check on the progress of the boys. By this time they should be able to set up

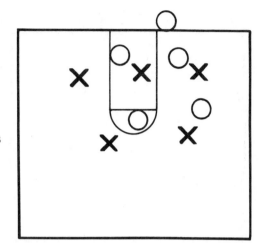

Figure 2-12. The 3-2 Zone Press

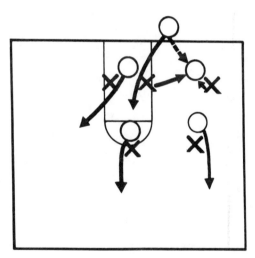

Figure 2-13. Attacking the 3-2 Press

properly against this sort of defense. If we note any errors, we correct them immediately.

After the pass-in to the nearest guard, the players break as shown in Fig. 2-13. We always want to go toward our offensive basket, but we also want to be in position to help the man with the ball whenever he's tied up by a double team.

Fig. 2-14 shows our set-up against a 2-2-1 zone press. Our players deploy a little differently than before; they're now in a loose 1-1-2-1. Though the first pass here is to the near man, in a game situation it would be determined by the reaction of the defense.

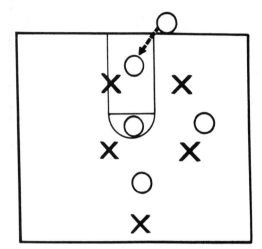

Figure 2-14. The 2-2-1 Zone Press

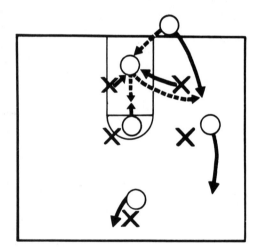

Figure 2-15. Attacking the 2-2-1 Zone Press

FIG. 2-15 shows the movement of the offensive players after the initial pass in-bounds. The thrower *goes opposite* his pass to replace the forward in the left lane, who has moved downcourt to clear out the defensive man in his area. The pivot man moves back a step to furnish help to the trapped player. The latter can throw to him or hit the out-of-bounds man who's now in the left lane. If he has a lot of time, he may be able to hit the forward breaking downcourt with a long pass.

The different options are there, and the boys must get used to finding them quickly under severe pressure. We want to move the ball downcourt as quickly as possible, as we feel that the ball must be moved faster than the defenders in order to get the odd-man situation we're looking for.

We know that it's easy to handle pressure verbally and on paper. The trick lies in equipping your boys with all of the requisite knowledge and skill, making them work as hard as they can to perfect it, and then hoping that they won't panic upon meeting pressure in a game situation.

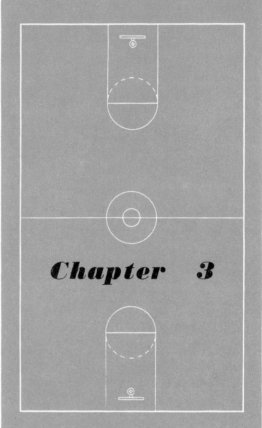

Chapter   3

ATTACKING
MAN-TO-MAN
PRESSURE

ONCE YOUR PLAYERS HAVE RECEIVED THE proper basic training, they should be ready to work on the actual methods of attacking the various types of pressure defense.

Our pressure attacks are based principally on the theories advanced in the preceding chapter. Whenever possible we look for the hole or weakness in the defense; we go immediately to the basket; we keep the ball moving forward; and we set up a series of posts. You'll find these principles implemented in nearly all of the attacking patterns that follow.

Photos 1-24. ATTACKING MAN-TO-MAN PRESSURE VIA THE DRIBBLE: The easiest and most effective way to destroy man-to-man pressure is with the dribble—if you have a strong enough, clever enough, cool enough, and fast enough dribbler. Just give him the ball, clear out, and let him go to work on his man. If you have an artist, like the boy in this sequence, the press shouldn't give you any trouble. The dribbler here capitalizes fully on his remarkable hands and

Photo 1

Photo 2

Photo 5

Photo 6

(continued) ambidextrous dribbling ability. He keeps his guard honest with a couple of quick, low dribbles in which he changes hands. He then starts his man to the right, dribbling low with his right hand. Once he has him moving, he abruptly puts on the brakes, switches the ball to his left hand, and drives hard down the opposite side. It's practically impossible to pressure such a dribbler one-on-one.

Photo 3

Photo 7

Photo 4

Photo 8

Attacking Man-to-Man Pressure Via the Dribble (cont.)

Photo 9   Photo 10

Photo 13   Photo 14

Photo 11   Photo 12

Photo 15   Photo 16

Attacking Man-to-Man Pressure Via the Dribble (cont.)

Photo 17   Photo 18

Photo 21   Photo 22

Photo 19 Photo 20

Photo 23 Photo 24

The simplest form of pressure you can expect to encounter is applied from the conventional man-to-man defense. The defensive team will keep leeching and harassing every attacker in an effort to wear down the offense and force it into committing such errors as wild passes, dropped passes, discontinued dribbles, steps, and charging.

There are several ways to attack the man-to-man pressure defense, depending upon your personnel.

Attack Via the Dribble

A skilled dribbler offers the simplest and frequently the best solution to the offensive problem. You just get him the ball, clear away from him, and turn him loose. By "clear away" I mean having the other offensive men take their defenders away from the ball so that none of them can double up on the dribbler. This is shown in FIG. 3-1.

The dribbler is allowed to bring the ball down-court on his own. Once he crosses the mid-court line, he has the option of driving toward the basket if he has beaten his man, or pulling up and setting up the team offense.

Attack Via a Post Series

If you have no skillful dribbler or if your dribbler cannot get the ball by the defense, you must use a post series to advance the ball, as shown in FIG. 3-2.

As before, the out-of-bounds man passes the ball in and cuts opposite. The receiver hits the first post man and also goes opposite into the outside fast-break lane. The first post hits the second post, and the latter can hit the deepest post or either man on the side. Note that all the fast break lanes have been filled.

By way of emphasis: After hitting the first post against the all-court man-to-man press, the out-of-bounds thrower should go opposite his pass in order to discourage his defensive man from double-teaming the receiver. The post man must be taught how to fake and feint so that he will be useful even when he is overplayed by the defensive opponent.

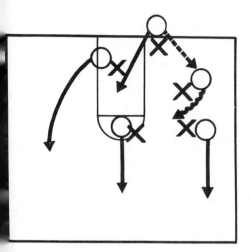

Figure 3-1. Pass-In and Clear-Out

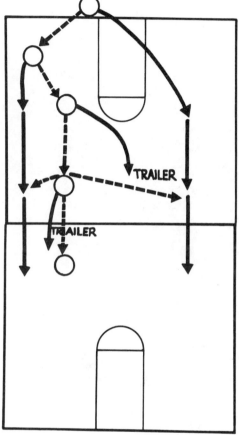

Figure 3-2. Post-Man Attack

Attacking the Switching Man-to-Man Press

The switching man-to-man press switches automatically with every cross of two offensive players. This type of press can be used either full-court or half-court, though it's generally more effective half-court where the coverage area is limited. We do not want our players to cross each other, with or without the ball, against the switching defense. This is exactly what the defense wants you to do. You'll be playing into their hands.

Photo 1

Photos 1-11. TWO-MAN SCREEN AND ROLL: The far attacker passes to the near man and follows the ball to set a screen on the receiver's guard (No. 3). The receiver fakes nicely to his left to distract his man, then moves sharply off the screen. The screener's guard (No. 20), anticipating the play, switches to the dribbler. The screener then pulls the perfect counter. The moment defensive man No. 3 hits him, he rolls for the basket. The dribbler, with a beautiful sweeping action off the top of his dribble, then hits the cutter with a lead bounce pass. Two steps and the receiver is in for the lay-up.

Photo 2

Photo 3

64

Photo 4

Photo 5

Photo 6

Photo 7

Photo 8

Photo 9

Photo 10

Photo 11

Photos 1-8. TWO-MAN GIVE-AND-GO: The far man fakes to his right, then cuts across for the pass from the near man. The latter brings his man down the side, then sharply cuts over him for the smart two-hand bounce pass from his teammate.

Photo 1

Photo 2

Photo 3

Photo 4

Two-Man Give-and-Go (cont.)

Photo 5

Photo 6

Photo 7

Photo 8

Photo 1

Photo 2

Photos 1-8. TWO-MAN GIVE-GO-AND-CHANGE: This is a highly effective counter against a switching man-to-man defense. The offensive idea against such a defense is not to cross. As you can see, the far attacker passes to the near man, and moves toward the receiver's guard (No. 3) as if to screen him. The other defensive man anticipates the screen and prepares to switch to the ball-handler. At this point the passer splits the two defensive men on a sharp cut for the basket, fouling up the switch. Note how he calls for the ball with his right hand and how the ball-handler delivers a nice lead lob pass.

Photo 3

Photo 4

Photo 5

Photo 6

Two-Man Give-Go-and-Change (cont.)

Photo 7

Photo 8

We go to an outside screening attack, as shown in Fig. 3-3. The outside moving screen takes the player into a position *behind* the defensive man. If the defender establishes any contact, regardless of how slight it is, the screener should immediately cut for the basket.

Fig. 3-3 shows the guard passing the ball to his guard teammate and then taking a moving screening position behind his teammate's defensive man. If the defenders switch, the screener cuts immediately to the basket. If there's no switch, the man with the ball can have a clear path to the basket on a drive over the screen. The middle has been cleared by the high post's outside-screening action for the forward.

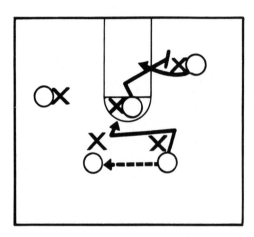

Figure 3-3. Half-Court Outside Screens

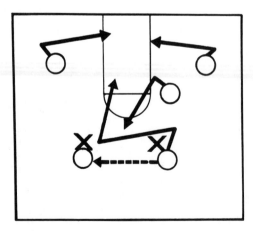

Figure 3-4. Give-and-Go Change of Direction

Fig. 3-4 shows a simple give-and-go change of direction based on the same principle of not crossing against the switching man-to-man pressure defense.

Summing up: To attack the switching man-to-man defense properly, you must be able to run your patterns with moving outside screens. Since there are so many surprise defenses, more stress should be placed on the type of offensive maneuvers (outside screens) that your team will be using during a ball game.

Freeing a Pressured Star

Every opponent will make a special effort to contain your star; and if you expect to get a maximum contribution from him you must prepare for every contingency. Your team must know exactly how to help their harassed teammate. The following pointers will help protect you from being devastated by the containment of a star player:

1. Teach your outstanding boy (high school level) to play several different positions.
2. Have him practice daily a good assortment of fakes and feints so that he will be extremely difficult to cover.
3. Develop a balanced offense so that if one individual is stopped the rest of the team can take up the slack.
4. Develop all of the boys on the team, not just the star player.
5. Mentally gear the star player for this type of pressure; don't let him get down on himself or quit during the game.
6. Design special screens for this situation.
7. Practice against this type of defense.
8. Stress the importance of the *team;* emphasize that any individual, no matter how good he is, is only part of the team.
9. Concentrate on feeding the star player before he is picked up by the defensive leech.
10. Run the defensive man into a good block early in the game. Make him aware of the fact that your team is setting screens for the star.

Fig. 3-5 shows how to set up screens for the pressured player. Assuming that he's being pressured all over the court and that he's your ball-handler, assign a specific player to screen the star's defen-

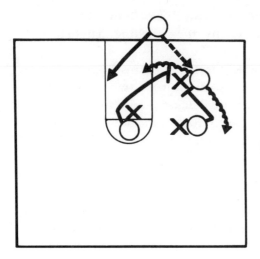

Figure 3-5. Screening a Pressured
Player in the Back-Court

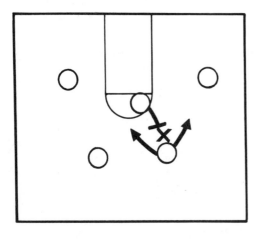

Figure 3-6. Screening a Pressured
Player in the Front-Court

sive man all the way down-court. Also have a nearby teammate come
over as an additional screen. The star then has the option of maneuvering in either direction. If he doesn't receive the pass, the screen
will generally force a defensive switch. This often is a help, as it takes
the outstanding defensive man away from your best offensive man
and weakens the defensive strategy.

Fig. 3-6 shows a screen for the man in the forecourt. Though the
high post man is doing the screening here, it can just as easily be
applied by a forward on the same side as the man being screened.
Our man can now go in either direction, depending upon the way
the opponent is guarding him. It's the offense's duty to screen for

its outstanding player and try to get him the ball as much as possible so that the attack won't be losing too much strength.

I've already mentioned the necessity for every team to be able to fast break. This is a good method of minimizing any sort of defensive pressure—attacking the defense before it can set up.

The Coach as a Sixth Player

A pressure defense sometimes becomes so harrowing to the players that coaches are compelled to call timeouts at awkward times in the game. The rules book recognizes this possibility and allows the coach to save himself several timeouts by permitting him to speak to his players from the bench.

Some coaches find this rule wonderful, as it allows them to communicate with their boys while the game is in progress. Other coaches feel that the coach should leave the boys alone while they're playing.

I believe in a happy medium. If the team needs help, it's the coach's duty to supply it. He just can't sit there and say nothing. It can easily cause a loss of respect from the players and a feeling that the coach isn't really in the game.

The coach is definitely needed on the high school level. Most schoolboy teams have only one expert ball-handler to bring the ball up; the other players are merely helpers. Since the pressure defense focuses on this one man, he must receive help and direction from the coach, particularly if he cannot handle the constant harassment. The coach's aid can be a life-saver to both the individual and the team as a whole. The coach must, however, do his coaching in a manner that won't embarrass his players in front of a crowd.

A smart coach can take a lot of pressure off the individual player. Where in the old days the ball-handling expert could size up the defense, bring the offense to a halt, and shout, "Zone! Zone! You play there, and you play there, etc.," nobody in the game today has the time or genius to decide what type of press the defense is using. With so many surprise pressures in force, the ball-handler can hardly be expected to diagnose the defense while he's being double- and triple-teamed. He has enough to worry about. The coach can be of tremendous help by immediately analyzing the defense and passing on the information to his players while the game is in progress.

Another good time to pass on information without calling a timeout is when your team is shooting a foul. Your players are generally back for defensive balance while the foul shooter is getting ready, and they can come over to the bench and converse with the coach.

The coach who has the respect of his players and can communicate with them can offer a great deal of help in a game, especially on the high school level. He can and should be the sixth man on the team during a ball game.

In the final analysis the key to breaking the various man-to-man pressure defenses lies in constant practice against it. This should be done daily. Your team should be ready for this type of pressure. Even in the years when you have weak personnel, you can improve your team by following general rules and practicing daily against all types of pressure. You can't win without good organization.

Also remember that there are many ways to skin a cat. It's up to you to select the methods and positioning that will best suit your team. You must make your players believe in your methods and philosophy. Once your team begins to execute successfully, they'll become solidly sold on your coaching techniques.

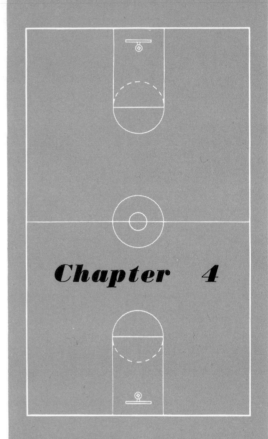

Chapter 4

IDENTIFYING
AND
ASSAYING
THE ZONE
PRESSES

WHERE THE MAN-TO-MAN PRESSURE DE-
fense is fairly simple to recognize, the
zone press comes in so many shapes
and forms that even the coach may
have trouble identifying the specific
variation. The failure to instantly
recognize it may have serious conse-
quences. The failure to meet it properly will usually mean defeat. That's
why every coach must prepare his boys
for any and all types of zone pressure.
The players must be so well prepared
and organized that they can make an
immediate adjustment to any surprise

defense. Planning helps to minimize the mistakes that the pressure defense continually tries to force.

The coach, as the sixth player on the team, represents the first line of assault. His natural impulse will be to call a timeout and diagnose the defense for the boys: "They are now in a zone. Let's switch to our zone offense." The impulse usually must be resisted. When the boys return to the floor, the opponents could well switch to another defense. The timeout will thus have been wasted.

The coach must be able to communicate with his team quickly and legally without calling a timeout. The team must know where he's sitting and must be geared to listen and look for help, if needed, and the coach must be able to come through with this help. It's essential whenever a team is under pressure and doesn't have the time to analyze the type of zone press that's being used against them.

The zone presses try to cause as much pressure as possible in order to get an individual or the entire team to crack. Your players must be so well prepared mentally and physically that they won't fall apart because of an occasional loss of the ball.

The substitute coming into the game cold and nervous can be a detriment to your club if he's not prepared for his job. Your best ball-handler is generally attacked. Where does he go? What does he do with the ball? Without the ball? How does he take the pressure? How can you steady the team? How do you avoid panic and confusion? How does your team control the pace of the game? How do you practice against a pressure defense?

These are some of the questions posed to the coach by a good zone press, and they can't be solved without having a thorough knowledge of every type of zone—their general objectives and their specific purpose at any stage in the game. Once you understand the purposes and objectives of all of these pressures, you must be able to pass this knowledge on to your players.

In organizing your work against pressure zones, place every type of zone that you know on a diagram sheet. From then on plan your attack by positioning your players on each diagram according to each man's strength and weaknesses. Each and every player must understand the fundamental way of deploying against the various types of zone pressures and understand that you may vary their positions depending on both their and the opponents' power.

We start by diagramming the zone press formations in half-court form, though the zone press is also used full-court and three-quarter court. We identify the different zone presses and pinpoint the weaknesses of each, as follows:

FIG. 4-1: the 1-2-2 Zone Press. The basic weaknesses or openings are the foul-line area or the sides. You must have patience and you must maneuver the ball to the area that you think will yield your best percentage shot. Your players must also be positioned according to their individual and overall strength.

FIG. 4-2: the 3-2 Zone Press. We overload both sides against this zone, as its weaknesses are along the sides and along the foul-line area. A high post on the foul line offers another way to combat this zone, as the middle area is open. It's desirable to use a man who can maneuver with the ball, not simply your biggest man.

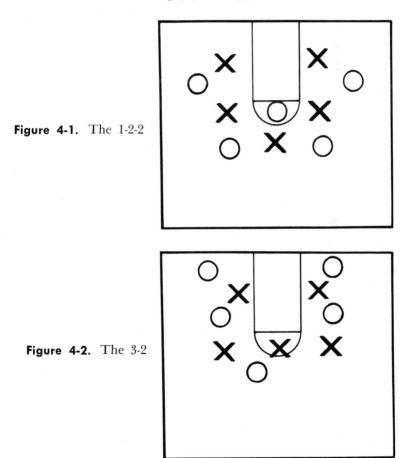

Figure 4-1. The 1-2-2

Figure 4-2. The 3-2

Fig. 4-3: the 2-3 Zone Press. The weakness is along the foul line and the sides of the foul line. We begin with the 1-3-1 attack and then maneuver our players according to the movement of the zone. Not all players think the same way or are capable of thinking the same way under pressure. They often need help, which should come from the other players or the coach (sixth man).

Fig. 4-4: the old conventional 2-1-2 Zone Press. This zone can be broken with either a 1-2-2 formation, as shown, or a 1-3-1 formation. The strengths of the zone lie in clogging the foul-line area and forc-

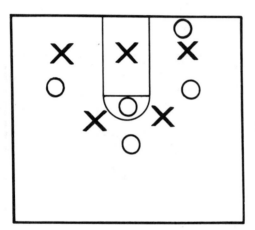

Figure 4-3. The 2-3

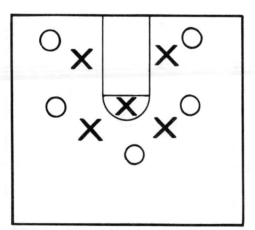

Figure 4-4. The 2-1-2

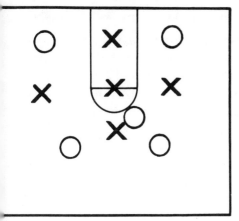

Figure 4-5. The 1-3-1

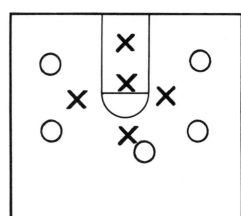

Figure 4-6. The 1-2-1-1

ing the offense to shoot from the sides. Its weakness is against a good outside shooting team. Since both side areas are open, the defenders under the basket must be able to cover both the side men and the men floating behind them from the corners to the basket.

In studying each formation, keep in mind the difference between positioning your players and actually penetrating the defense. In the past the zone defense would hold their positions. Today's zonemen, however, automatically change positions from zone to zone according to the movement of the offensive players. The offensive team and coach must be able to make immediate positional adjustments with each defensive change. The holes and openings will always be there; the trick is to get your players to find them in the quickest and surest way possible.

Fig. 4-5: the 1-3-1 Zone Press. Originally this zone was designed to defense the big man. Its prime purpose was to have a man in front of and a man behind the big center at all times. The other thought was always to have three men in line with the ball and the basket. Its weaknesses are the corners and a high post man at the top of the key. The attack against this type of zone remains a 2-1-2.

Fig. 4-6: the 1-2-1-1 Zone Press. This defense takes away your strength down the middle, but is extremely weak down the sides and in the corners. We attack it with a 1-2-2 set-up.

It should be understood that our attacking formation in most instances is flexible. Aside from the fact that every zone keeps changing formations with the movement of the offensive players, they'll sometimes set up in a certain formation in order to force you to position your men in the conventional manner. They'll then change suddenly and completely to hit you with a quick double- or triple-team attack.

You must always have your players prepared for the surprise change of defense. You can do this by assigning certain players as outlet pass men in case of a sneak attack. It's their duty to come and get the ball from the trapped teammate.

FIG. 4-7: the 3-1-1 Zone Press. The weakness of this defense is down the sides and the corners. It has often been used with three big men up front, who challenge the offensive ball-handlers to see or throw over them. Michigan used three big men up front to overcome a big deficit against the great Bill Bradley Princeton team. They forced the Princeton backcourt men and ball-handlers into constant errors trying to see and pass over the big Michigan pressure front line.

FIG. 4-8: the 2-2-1 Zone Press. The weaknesses here lie down the middle in the foul line area and the corners.

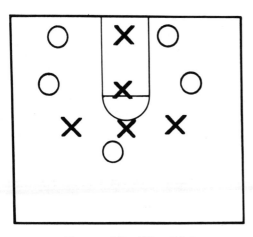

Figure 4-7. The 3-1-1

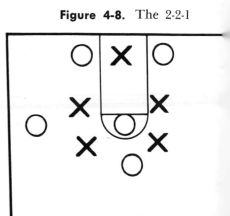

Figure 4-8. The 2-2-1

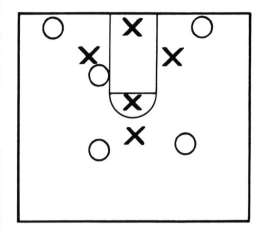

Figure 4-9. The 1-1-2-1

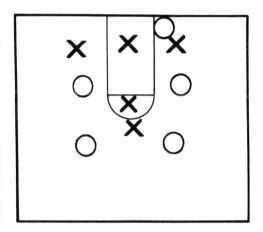

Figure 4-10. The 1-1-3

FIG. 4-9: the 1-1-2-1 Zone Press. This defense's immediate weaknesses are the corner areas and the outside area (ball-handling area 25 feet out). The two back men in the 2-1-2 offensive alignment can, by spreading, force the top man into covering a lot of territory. The offense will thus shoot primarily from the outside and the corners.

FIG. 4-10: the 1-1-3 Zone Press. Its weaknesses are either on top outside or on the outside along the foul-line area. This is another zone that will cause the offensive team to shoot from the outside.

In setting up against these zone pressure defenses, you must place your boys in the most vulnerable positions of the particular type of zone used. You must also understand that with the great variety of shifting in each zone you had better prepare your boys to shoot from all areas. You cannot say, "Well, since we don't have any outside shooter, we're sunk." You must devise the method of attacking each zone that's most adaptable to your team.

The method you use will depend on the specific zone used by the opposition. Your team must have a thorough understanding of their fundamental positioning against every type of zone pressure defense. Though you would think it would be more difficult to attack a pressure zone in a confined area (half-court), zone teams such as UCLA and St. Joseph's have been extremely successful using it full-court. This takes a combination of good planning, expert teaching and organization, and quick, alert, smart, aggressive, and outstanding ballplayers.

It makes very little difference what style you use to break the different types of zone pressure. The openings remain in the same areas, and whether you decide to use a rotation or a stationary system or to send cutters through the zone, the good pressure defense will still give you only the shots they're willing to yield. Their defense is designed to give you this shot. It's your job to get your team ready for every one of these defenses and to shoot from the different areas of the court under different pressure situations.

General Rules and Principles

After we've finished instructing our boys on positioning and actually get into working on the floor, we lay down a set of rules that we want the boys to observe most of the time. These rules are broken down into simple terms so that the players will have no great problem understanding what we want.

1. Position yourself in areas away from the defensive players. (If the zone changes, be alert and move to a new clear area.)
2. Force the defense to attack the ball at a point that we want them to. (Dribble right to the area where you want to be attacked.)
3. Always make progress with the ball; don't pass laterally unless absolutely necessary for safety.
4. Always *look up-court* before dribbling or passing.
5. Always look for the odd-man advantage (three-on-two, etc.) and take the shot.

6. Try to spread the defense as much as possible; make them cover as much of the court as possible.

7. Let the defensive team know that you can ball-handle by passing the ball around several times while trying to penetrate for a shot.

8. Take good shots only. Don't rush a shot. You can always get a bad or forced shot.

9. Always maintain your team defensive balance.

10. Try to avoid dribbling against the zone presses; do it only if necessary.

11. When dribbling always be aware that you're being chased and will probably be attacked on the blind side.

12. Move the ball before the double-team is effected.

13. Fake before passing.

14. Get the ball in over the end line quickly before the press forms.

15. Always go away from the man that you pass to; don't bring another defensive man into a clogged area.

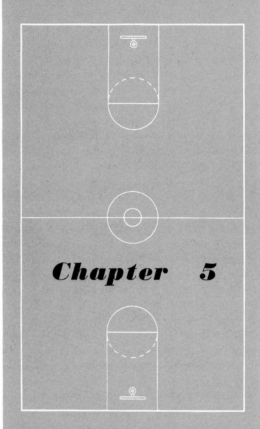

Chapter 5

ATTACKING
FULL-COURT
ZONE
PRESSURE

HAVING SHOWED OUR PLAYERS THE proper positioning against the different zone press formations, and made certain that they know where the weaknesses of each zone are, we go into the full-court zone press attack.

We feel very strongly about the importance of attacking the press aggressively. We *must* look for the free man after being double- and triple-teamed, and we must capitalize on this free man advantage (we call it the odd-man advantage). The diagrams that follow will show how to attack every

Photo 1

Photos 1-19. BREAKIN[
THE FULL-COURT ZON
PRESS: This remarkable s
quence shows a full-scale o
eration against the zone pres
The out-of-bounds man hi
the ace ball-handler and go
opposite (to fill the near si
lane). The receiver hesitates
moment to draw the two ir
mediate pressers to him, th
fires a bounce pass to a po
man set up above the lan
The post man turns and loo
for another post near mi
court or for the first pass
coming up the side. Findir
the latter open, he hits hi
with the ball. The latter the
fires to the man in the midd.
who dribble-drives for the o
posite lane. The last pho
shows the three-on-two sitt
tion that develops in the sc
ing lane.

Photo 2

Photo 3

94

Photo 4

Photo 5

Photo 6

Photo 7

Breaking the Full-Court Zone Press (cont.)

Photo 8

Photo 9

96

Photo 10

Photo 11

Photo 12

Photo 13

**Breaking the Full-Court
Zone Press (cont.)**

Photo 14

Photo 15

Photo 16

Photo 17

Photo 18

Photo 19

Photo 1   Photo 2

Photos 1-6. PASS AND GO OP-
POSITE: This is the originating
point of the entire pressure offense
and must be thoroughly mastered
for the attack to have any chance of
succeeding. The out-of-bounds man
must wait for his near teammate
(the team's best ball-handler) to
shake loose from the pressuring
guards. He then hits him with the
pass and immediately goes (breaks)
opposite. If the defensive men stay
with the ball, the receiver looks for
a quick return pass to his breaking
teammate. Its frequently smart to
wait for the double-team before
passing off, as this will immediately
eliminate two pressing defenders.

Photo 4

100

Photo 3

Photo 5   Photo 6

zone press, always assuming that the defense will double-team the
initial movement of the ball.

Attacking the 1-2-2

FIG. 5-1 shows the line-up against the 1-2-2 full-court zone press,
whose weakness lies in the middle of the court. The out-of-bounds
man has the option of passing to No. 2 or No. 4. The defense here
permits the throw-in to No. 2, who's immediately double-teamed
by X1 and X2.

Since we want No. 2 to draw two men to him, we tell him to delay
after receiving the ball until he's attacked by two men. This leaves
the defense with only three men to cover the entire court, while we
have four—giving us the desired odd-man advantage. No. 1, after passing from out of bounds, always goes opposite his pass, but looks back
to see if No. 2 needs help.

The next pass goes from No. 2 to No. 4. Meanwhile, No. 5 takes
off down-court to set a high post in case No. 4 wants to hit him with
the next pass. Almost all of the attacks against a zone press should
make constant use of post men. Even if they're not used, they must
be ready to help out the players who are being double- and triple-
teamed.

Notice in the diagram that all of the players always *go away* from
the man who receives the ball. This is in keeping with our principle
of spreading the court, giving the defense more coverage and filling
our fast-break lanes.

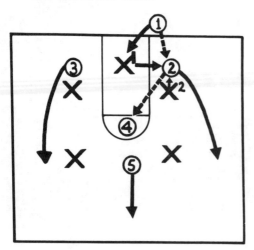

Figure 5-1. Attacking the 1-2-2

Attacking the 3-2 Zone Press

Our method of penetrating the 3-2 zone press is quite similar to our attack against the 1-2-2. The in-bounds pass goes to No. 2 or No. 4, if possible. FIG. 5-2 shows it going to No. 2. Since the weakness of this zone also lies down the middle, we direct our passes to this area. No. 2 passes to No. 4 and then follows the principle of going opposite the ball and filling one of the three fast-break lanes. No. 4 has the option of passing to No. 5 or either No. 3 or No. 2, both of whom are in the outside lanes going down the floor.

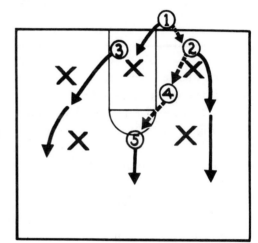

Figure 5-2. Attacking the 3-2

We realize that it's easy to do all of this in a diagram. The trick is to get your boys to make all of these movements quickly and safely. In order to do this they must follow the principles that you've established versus the zone press.

Attacking the 2-3 Zone Press

The weakness of the 2-3 zone lies down the middle, and its penetration is begun with an in-bounds pass to No. 3, as shown in FIG. 5-3. If No. 3 is covered, No. 1 has the option of passing to No. 2 or No. 5. No. 3 passes to post man No. 5. During this passing sequence, No. 4 has gone down-court to set a post for a pass from No. 5. No. 2 fills an

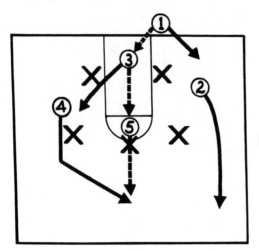

Figure 5-3. Attacking the 2-3

outside fast-break lane while No. 3, after passing to No. 5, fills the opposite fast-break lane.

Again notice the implementation of our principles of going away from the pass, setting up posts, and filling the fast-break lanes. No. 1 becomes the defensive balance man. If the others cannot make their outlet pass because of a double-team, he is back there for a safety pass.

The remainder of our diagrams will detail all of our maneuvers without any further brainwashing on principles and rules and regulations. By now I'm sure that all of you understand what we're trying to do.

Attacking the 2-1-2 Zone Press

Our attack versus the 2-1-2 starts with No. 1's inbound pass to No. 2. (Fig. 5-4.) Since the weakness of this zone is along the sides, No. 2 passes over to No. 4 and then fills the left fast-break lane. No. 3 replaces No. 5 as the high post and becomes the target for No. 4. The latter can pass either to No. 3, as in the diagram, or take the ball down the floor himself in the right lane. No. 5 meanwhile has broken down court to take one of the defensive men with him or to make himself available as another post. The three fast-break lanes have been filled by No. 2 (left lane), No. 4 (right lane), and No. 5 (in the middle).

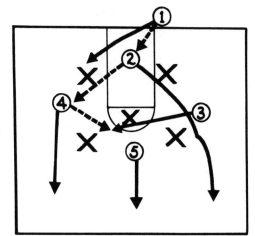

Figure 5-4. Attacking the 2-1-2

Attacking the 1-3-1 Zone Press

Our attack against the 1-3-1 is launched with an inbounds pass to No. 2, as shown in Fig. 5-5. Since the weaknesses of this zone normally are the sides, No. 2 then hits No. 4. Meanwhile, No. 5 sets a post for No. 4, if it is needed. No. 3 fills the right fast-break lane, No. 4 fills the left lane, and No. 5 the middle, with No. 1 and No. 2 coming up the court as the trailers.

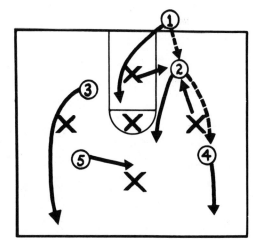

Figure 5-5. Attacking the 1-3-1

Attacking the 1-2-1-1 Zone Press

The weaknesses of the 1-2-1-1 zone are down the sides, as it concentrates on clogging the middle. As shown in Fig. 5-6, we throw in to No. 2. If he's double-teamed, we'll bring back No. 3 and just reverse our procedure to the opposite side of the court. No. 2 looks down his side of the court and passes to No. 4. Meanwhile, No. 3 has become the middle man, as No. 5 has broken down-court toward the basket, taking the last defender with him.

No. 1, who took the ball out of bounds, has a long run to become the third man down the right fast-break lane. He must hustle all the way. No. 4 has the option of passing to No. 3, as shown, dribbling down himself, or passing to No. 5 if he's free.

You've probably noticed that in most of our plays, No. 5 is sent down-court after we establish our initial movements with the ball. Being farthest away from the ball, it's easy for him to penetrate deep. If we can eventually get him the ball down-court, even on a long gambling pass, against most types of zone pressure he'll be left with one man and have a good one-on-one situation.

This option depends on your personnel and whether you want No. 5 to be your big man. The tall fellow won't be able to maneuver as well as your other players, or be an exceptionally good one-on-one player.

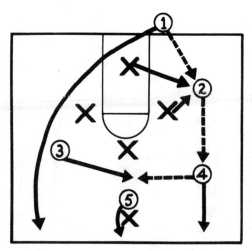

Figure 5-6. Attacking the 1-2-1-1

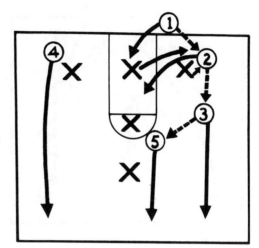

Figure 5-7. Attacking the 3-1-1

Attacking the 3-1-1 Zone Press

The 3-1-1 zone takes the middle away from you, but is vulnerable at the sides. As shown in Fɪɢ. 5-7, we penetrate by moving our initial passes up the side. Once the zone has to shift positions, we can make use of our post men. No. 1 throws to No. 2, who must move to the ball. If the latter is closely guarded, No. 3 and No. 4 must come back. The ensuing movement is determined by which man receives the outlet pass. All the players must be alert to fluxes in the situation.

If No. 2 can get the throw-in, he hits No. 3 down the side with the next pass. The latter can either dribble down-court or pass to No. 5, the high post, and then take the fast-break lane down the left side. No. 4 fills the right fast-break lane. No. 1 becomes a safety receiver if No. 2 can't get the ball to No. 3, while No. 2, after passing to No. 3, trails down the middle to help No. 5 if he becomes stuck with the ball.

Attacking the 2-2-1 Zone Press

The weaknesses of the 2-2-1 are along the sides and the foul-line area. As shown in Fɪɢ. 5-8, our initial pass goes to No. 2, who then hits post man No. 4 and takes the fast-break lane down the left side. No. 4 hits No. 5, who assays the situation down the court and either drives or passes ahead.

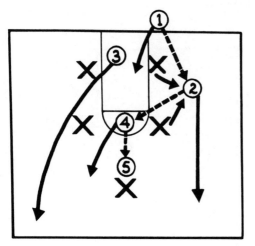

Figure 5-8. Attacking the 2-2-1

No. 3, who didn't receive the out-of-bounds pass, now becomes the opposite fast-break wing man. No. 1 trails the play as a safety-valve, helping out if either No. 2 or No. 4 are trapped in a double-team.

Attacking the 1-1-2-1 Zone Press

The 1-1-2-1 is strong in the middle, but weak at the sides. It lets the offense get the ball in to No. 2, then hits him with a double-team.

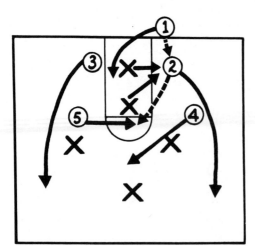

Figure 5-9. Attacking the 1-1-2-1

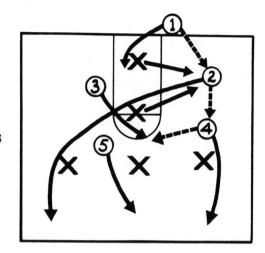

Figure 5-10. Attacking the 1-1-3

As shown in Fig. 5-9, No. 5 comes across to set a post and receive the ball from No. 2. No. 1 becomes the safety man for No. 2. The latter has the option of returning the ball to No. 1 when attacked, or hitting No. 4 or No. 3.

After No. 5 receives the pass, No. 4 breaks toward the middle to become the next post man. By now No. 3 has filled the right fast-break lane and No. 2 the left lane. No. 5 has the option of passing to No. 4 on the post or hitting either No. 3 or No. 2 in the fast-break lanes. He can also hand the ball back to the safety valve, No. 1.

Attacking the 1-1-3 Zone Press

Like the 1-1-2-1, the 1-1-3 zone is strong in the middle and weak at the sides. We attack it as shown in Fig. 5-10. The ball is passed in to No. 2 along the side, who in turn passes to No. 4. No. 2 then fills the right fast-break lane. No. 5, meanwhile, breaks down-court to clear out his defensive man. He becomes a post down-court.

No. 3 breaks from his position to the top of the circle for a pass from No. 4, his side of the court being filled by No. 2. No. 4, after passing to No. 3, fills in the left fast-break lane. No. 1 again becomes a safety valve; we look for him when in trouble or when we cannot get the odd-man situation with the other four men.

Changing Up on the Defense

Since we use different men in different positions in each of these formations it's important to understand our thinking. We feel that if the defensive team can change defenses on us, why can't we change up on them? Our boys are thus prepared to play a variety of positions and to fill different lanes in going down-court.

The switching of offensive positions from time to time has other advantages. It prevents your attack from becoming stereotyped and thus easily "read." Neither the opposing coach nor the scout in the stands can say, "Each player always goes to the exact same spot and all we have to do is take their set positions away."

The interchanging of positions is thus most important. During your early season practices, teach your boys to play as many different positions as possible. Your job is to use them in the manner that best helps the team. There are exceptions, of course. You don't want to move the very big boy or the very little boy around too much. But these are extremes.

On the high school level most boys can be taught to play guard, forward, and center. Most teams are of average size and you'll seldom see a very big team on which every boy is a specialist. On the college level, where boys are hand-picked by the coach, you're more apt to find a specialist at each position.

Diagrams Don't Provide All the Answers

My attempt here has been to establish simple but effective attacking patterns against the various types of zone presses. I realize that there are endless variations of both defense and offense, but I believe that these patterns can comprise an excellent fundamental attack for coaches on every level of competition.

Having read a good many books myself over the past 15 years, I know that almost everything looks good on paper. Unfortunately, many of these brilliant maneuvers break down when used against moving players. The diagram cannot show hands waving on defense, bothering your players. It cannot show exceptional defensive players —quick, alert, aggressive men. It cannot show three giants pressuring a little man so that he cannot get his initial pass off. It cannot show how a player or team panics when they lose the ball a few times.

I realize this and you, as the reader, should also realize this. The diagrams are intended to help you set your players in the right positions and to show you a sound progression of moves. From that point on you had better have well-trained players who know their fundamentals and who are prepared to carry out their assignments as they learned and practiced them in your workouts.

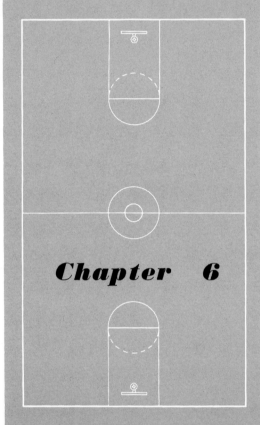

Chapter   6

ATTACKING SPECIAL PRESSURE DEFENSES

NOT TOO MANY YEARS AGO IT WAS fairly simple to plan an attack against a coming opponent. When a team came out in either a man-to-man defense or some form of zone, such as 2-1-2, 1-3-1, 2-3, or 3-2, you could expect them to stay in it. All you had to do was position your players to the best advantage against the particular defense and then hope you made your shots.

Today the attacking problem is far more complex. Most teams play a variety of zone defenses, and will

sometimes throw all of them at you in one game. For some reason
the zone holds terror for most boys. Your first job, therefore, is a
selling one. You must sell your boys on the fact that it's easier to
play against a zone, where they're not hounded all the time, than
against a man-to-man defense that continually dogs each player. If
you can sell your team on this and make them look forward to playing against zone defenses, chances are they'll have better success
against them.

The difficulty starts after you've brainwashed your team against
the zone defense. They now understand all the principles of attacking the various zones, then suddenly they're hit with a special defense
—the Box-and-One, or the Diamond-and-One or Triangle-and-One.
Both of these defenses are geared to stop an outstanding player, or
to put as much pressure on him as possible to keep him from having
his average game.

Then there's the combination defense. This is partly man-to-man
and partly zone. It can be set up with two men playing man-to-man
and three playing a zone, or three playing man-to-man and two playing a zone. Numerous other combinations are possible, none of
which take a set or static form. This places a lot of pressure on both
the coach and the players. You never know exactly what you're going
to come up against.

Most coaches agree that penetration is essential against every type
of zone, since the zone not only reacts to the movement of the ball
around the floor, but follows the movement of the players as well.
If your players stand around instead of moving against the zone
(cutting and screening), they'll have a difficult time against these
defenses. They won't be working for the good shot, and probably
won't penetrate the defense enough to win.

As recently as 15 years ago, most coaches wouldn't cut against the
zone. They wanted their boys to hold their positions and concentrate on ball-handling and passing. Such things as screens were un-
heard of. The advent of the modern zone has changed all this thinking. The coach must now combat the zone with both *ball movement*
and *player movement*. The attacking team *must* be able to do both.

It's understood, of course, that if you're playing against a defense
that your boys can break without difficulty and without extra movement, you can still use the old method of standing around in assigned

positions. As a rule, however, you won't have much success standing around. You'll permit part of the defense to play you man-to-man, while the rest of the defense double- and triple-teams the man with the ball.

In breaking special defenses, it's important to know all of the different zones that we've discussed in the previous chapter. The players must be well-schooled on your principles and rules and must know what types of shots to look for against the different zones.

Attacking the Box-and-One

The box-and-one is one of the most troublesome zone defenses for the high school coach. Almost every high school team has just one boy who does the bulk of the scoring, and it's on this boy that the defense heavily concentrates. One defensive player is assigned to cover him man-to-man. This guard will generally stick to him all over the court and try to stop him from receiving the ball. The other four defensive men will play a zone. Wherever the outstanding boy goes, he's running into some zone area. He now not only has a personal guard to worry about, but he's picking up another defensive man along the way.

You have a decision to make. In planning your attack, you must decide whether to sacrifice your exceptional player or attempt to free him so that he can make his usual contribution to the team. I feel that a team must be able to do both these things. If your only aim is to free the boy, you'll always lose against a strong defense that stops him. In fact even if he scores his share, the other players will still have to do their share in order to win the game.

The better idea is to develop an attack which has the outstanding player being helped by his teammates and he in turn helping them. The first weapon against the box-and-one should, whenever possible, be the fast break. Many zone players tend to linger before running back to their starting positions and will thus be vulnerable to a quick breaking attack. The zone generally requires all of the defensive men to be in position before it can function properly. If you get down-court ahead of them, chances are they'll be opening for the good percentage shot. Every team should know how and when to fast break.

To free the outstanding player against the box-and-one, you must get him into a one-on-one situation. Perhaps the best way to do this is by playing him on the high post along the foul line, as shown in Fig. 6-1. As you can see, you've now forced the defensive formation into a 3-2 zone. The strategy then is to break the zone with the use of your outstanding player. You can now overload areas, etc. If you feed your man on the high post, he can attempt either to maneuver his man or find the free man if the defense is concentrating more than one man on him.

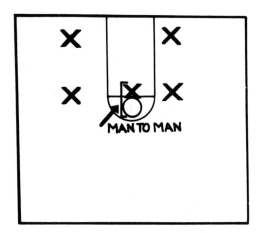

Figure 6-1. Box-and-One

You can readily see that the zone will automatically change according to the area in which the offensive player decides to position himself. Your players should understand this and break the zone according to the principles they've been taught in practice.

The outstanding player should always attempt to position himself so that he'll always have a one-on-one situation whenever he receives the ball. The exceptional player can use teammates for screens. Since he's usually followed blindly by his watchdog, a teammate can easily set a standing screen for him. Once the defensive hound is screened several times, he'll become more aware of what's going on around him and probably will lessen his concentration on the player.

Another method of beating this particular defense is for the star to sacrifice himself in order to get better shots for his teammates.

There usually will be many opportunities for him to set up his team-mates for nice easy short shots, as the defense will be gambling on them. The free teammates must take their shots. This is why every boy should be worked into all of the daily practice drills. If your first team gets all of the work and all of the plays are designed for one boy, you can hardly expect a boy who doesn't have much experience shooting the ball in practice or playing with the members of the first team to walk onto the court and get the job done.

On most of the one-on-one situations in this attack, the boy may be playing with his back to the basket or cutting from one side of the court to the other. In most instances he'll be moving without the ball. He must depend on his teammates to get him the ball. If he's a guard who's used to playing the backcourt, he'll have a much more difficult time unless he learns how to play with his back to the basket.

It's not difficult to teach an *outstanding* boy to play both facing the basket and with his back to it. He must learn how to play a variety of positions, as he's sure to catch a lot of special defenses, par-ticularly if he's your key player.

Attacking the Diamond-and-One Defense

The diamond or triangle-and-one defense is also designed against an individual player, and calls for the same kind of attack that was given for the box-and-one defense. Fig. 6-2 shows the alignment of this particular defense. The defensive players are set up in diamond shape with one man at the top of the circle, two men on either side

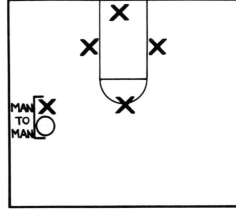

Figure 6-2. Diamond-and-One

of the lane under the foul line, and the fourth (generally the biggest and best rebounder) under the basket. The fifth man is assigned to follow the outstanding boy all over the court.

Once again, as against the box-and-one, the offensive players will deploy according to where the outstanding boy sets up initially. The zone will then assume a more familiar shape to the players. FIG. 6-3 will give you an idea of what happens to the zone when the outstanding boy posts himself along the foul line. The zone now appears to be a 1-3-1. Your team can then proceed to break that particular formation. Actually what we're trying to do is force the opponents to play the type of zone that we want them to.

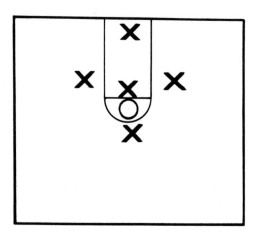

Figure 6-3. Forcing the Diamond to Change

In your pre-game planning you should know which players are most effective against the different zones and attempt to force the defense into that type of zone. It isn't necessary to draw any additional diagrams. FIGS. 6-1 and 6-3 graphically show how the position of the one boy can force the defensive team into a different zone.

Attacking the Combination Defense

We now know that we want ball movement and player movement. We also know that we want to be the aggressors on attack. We want the zone to shape up according to the way we position or move the ball and players.

Let's assume that the opponents go into a combination defense as the ball is brought down the floor, with the guards playing man-to-man and the three back men (forwards and center) forming a triangle zone defense (Fig. 6-4). If you attack it as you would a 2-1-2 zone, you'll be in trouble. The so-called chasers up front won't stand there. They'll pick a man (one taking the ball and the other taking the backcourt man without the ball) and play them man-to-man all over the floor or only up to a certain part of the floor. This defense is geared to keep your rebounders in a certain area, and to confuse and disrupt the planned attack.

The offensive team may not know whether they're facing a man-to-man or a zone, and may be unable to decide whether to break it with a zone offense or a man-to-man offense. The defense may also be trained to switch on signals (hand, ball, or direction of the ball or key player), so that by the time the offensive team decides how to attack the defense they may be pretty far behind in the score.

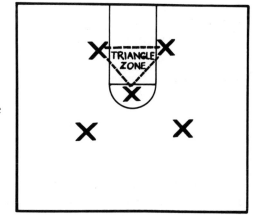

Figure 6-4. Combination Zone and Man-to-Man

We've found that the best offense against this defense is a regular man-to-man attack. We treat the defense like a man-to-man and attempt to move the ball and the players. The danger lies in turn-overs and poor defensive balance, and we make our players aware of this. With patience and movement, we'll get the open shots if the triangle sticks to the zone principle—as we have two men cutting

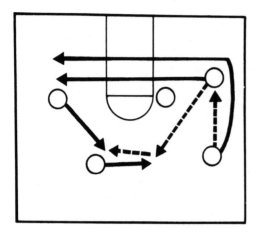

Figure 6-5. Movement Against Combination Defense

across court behind the triangle to overload a side. This is shown in FIG. 6-5. The defense will have to maneuver quickly and smartly to follow the two cutters.

With good ball-handling, your best shooters should be getting the most shots from the best percentage area. All of this is fine, provided you have some boys who can shoot straight. Heaven help you if you don't have any boys who can put the ball into the hoop with any consistency.

Out-of-Bounds Attack

Every team should have several out-of-bounds plays with which to hit the pressure defense. A good play can alleviate the pressure and give the attack a desperately needed basket and boost in morale.

The chief out-of-bounds areas lie under the offensive basket and along the side line. The defense may differ considerably in these areas. The man taking the ball out under the offensive hoop normally won't be attacked, as he has the end line for protection and knows exactly what he's going to do. On an outside play along the side line, you can expect the guard taking the thrower to drop off and help double-team the logical receiver.

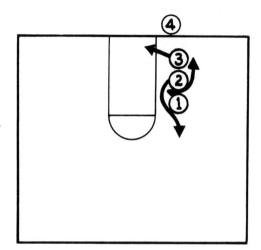

Figure 6-6. Out-of-Bounds Play

• *Under the Basket*

A team should have no more than two plays or just one with several options against a normal man-to-man pressure defense. It's unwise to have your boys memorize and learn too many of these plays. You don't want them to have to stop and think when they have only five seconds to execute the play.

FIG. 6-6 shows a good under-the-basket play against the man-to-man. Player 1 fakes one step toward the basket and then cuts closely behind Nos. 2 and 3 for a pass from No. 4 for the short jump shot. If No. 3's man switches, No. 3 goes directly to the basket for a pass from No. 4. No. 2, after the screen, drops back for a safety pass, while No. 5 takes his man away from the play. If No. 5's man lays back to help out the others, No. 4 has the option of making the quick pass to No. 5 for his shot.

If the opponent's zone presses to stop you from cutting, run the play the same way in an effort to shake a man free, or you can be satisfied just to get the ball into play safely and then start your zone offense, os shown in FIG. 6-7.

The defense has now lined up three big men with arms outstretched about three feet from the basket. They prevent any offensive players from getting in front of them under the basket and make it as difficult as they can for the thrower to see over them and pass the ball to a cutter. The other two defensive men clog the three-second area. This sometimes can be done by just one of them, with the other player setting up near the foul line or top of the circle in order to intercept a long safety pass.

As I stated before, you can still try to force the defense to follow the cutters. Or you can get the ball inbounds safely by deploying your men in screening position for the two deepest men and then throwing in to one of the other free men, as shown in FIG. 6-7.

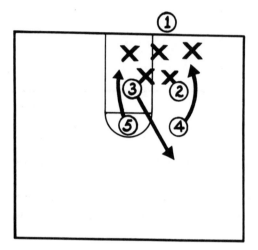

Figure 6-7. Out-of-Bounds vs Zone Pressure

Players 2 and 3 screen for Nos. 4 and 5. If No. 1 can get the ball to No. 4 quickly, he should. His pass should be over the outstretched arms and jumping defenders. The pass that we want is for safety, not for the shot. If we get the shot, good, but we still want the ball whether we get the shot or not. If the pass isn't there, No. 5, on the signal, cuts by No. 3 in an attempt to make No. 3's man go with him. No. 4 does the same in cutting by No. 2. No. 3 will then break far outside behind No. 2's screen as the safety valve.

- *Along the Side Line*

Before working any play it's essential to get the ball in safely within the five-second period. We again need movement and screening to avoid the double-team by the guard playing the out-of-bounds man. As shown in Diag. 6-8, the center or forward assumes a high post position, with guards screening for each other if necessary. After the ball is brought in safely, we can attack from a balanced offensive position.

FIG. 6-9 shows the popular three-man line-up on an out-of-bounds ball from the side. A play can be worked from this line-up or you can be content with just the safety pass inbounds, depending on your evaluation of the situation. Every team should have at least one spe-

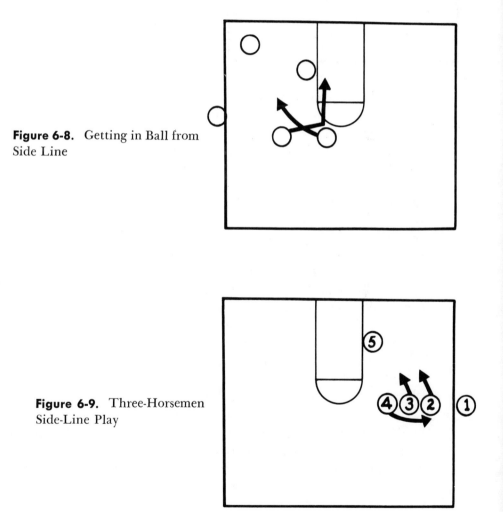

Figure 6-8. Getting in Ball from Side Line

Figure 6-9. Three-Horsemen Side-Line Play

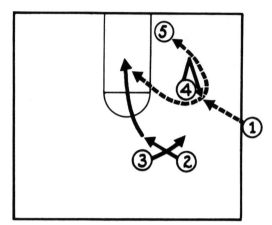

Figure 6-10. Side-Line Special

cial play for the end of the half after a timeout has been called with just seconds to play. The team should know how many seconds it takes to run their play and operate accordingly. You definitely don't want to give the ball back to the other side for a last shot before time runs out.

The side-line set-up (FIG. 6-9) is a good one for this situation. Upon a given signal Nos. 2 and 3 screen for No. 4. If there's a switch by X2 or X3, the screeners must immediately cut toward the basket. Depending on the way the defensive team lines up, you may have a one-on-one situation for No. 5. If he's a good, agile player, it would be best to throw him the ball directly from the out-of-bounds area.

If the opponents are in a zone press, you must pass the ball in strictly for safety, then go into the high post series, as shown in FIG. 6-10. The type of pressure being applied will determine the pass —whether No. 4 passes to No. 5 for a one-on-one situation, or to No. 2 cutting to the basket, or back out to No. 3 to set up the zone pressure attack.

Regardless of what type of play you use or whatever your purpose is, there must be options and variations off the one or two plays. The simpler you make the game, the easier it will be for *the players* to comprehend. It's execution that makes any offensive or defensive maneuver successful.

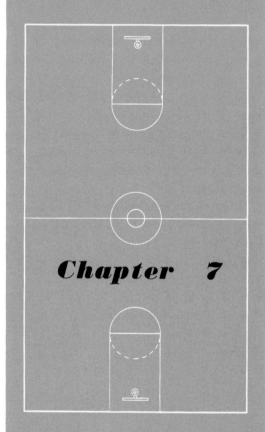

Chapter *7*

PHILOSOPHY
AND
TEAM
ORGANIZATION

TO ACHIEVE SUCCESS AGAINST THE PRESsure or any other kind of defense, you must gird your boys, both mentally and physically, for a 100% effort. These preparations must be begun long before your boys ever step onto the floor. Indeed, the roots of their mental and physical indoctrination lie in the coach's philosophy or approach to the game.

Every coach must develop specific objectives that he should pass on to his players. He should make sure they understand the objectives and how he intends to achieve them. In short the coach must tell his players exactly what he will attempt to do.

The truly responsible coach understands that he has something more to offer than fun, exercise, and glory. He understands that he spends an unusual amount of time with his boys, that he has something they want, that he can lead and motivate them, and that he has the opportunity to develop them both on and off the court.

Though it's sometimes difficult to control the boys away from the floor, the dedicated coach will make the attempt. The good he does off the court can frequently be more meaningful than his actual coaching. He should be interested not only in bodies, but in minds and hearts as well. This sort of coach will be long remembered by his boys for what he stood for and what he tried to get through to them while they were going through their growing stages.

The question arises: "How can you do all of these things?"

My answer is: take an interest in every boy on your squad. Not just the regulars, but also the substitutes, the managers, and everyone else in the program. They all want and need the same thing—recognition.

You can't fake this sort of interest. The modern kid is sensitive to insincerity, and he can spot the "phoney" immediately. That means you must be circumspect in all your dealings with the players. Your door must remain open to all of them so that they can come to you with their problems. The more you help them, the more you will sell yourself, the closer will be your rapport, and the more you will get out of them.

Your philosophy will dictate how you act and how you dispatch your duties. I believe that every boy should leave your school a better and more informed person who is capable of saying, "If I had a brother, or when I have a son, I'd like him to play for that man."

You can never stop working on your objectives and ideals. To get them across to everyone in the program, you must work at it from year to year, month to month, and day to day—never letting the boys forget what is expected of them.

This doesn't always come easy. Almost every squad will have its problem child or children. This very small percentage will fight you and refuse to conform to the thinking of the group. You must work harder with this type of boy. It's obvious that he has a problem, and his future happiness may sometimes hinge on the way you handle it.

You will always know when you're getting across to your players. It will manifest itself in the team attitude, the team spirit, and how the boys react to both winning and losing efforts.

You must represent authority. You must be able to answer any questions on the technical phases of the game, and you must display leadership every day—both in practice and during the emotional stress of competition.

Players have a tendency to imitate their coach, especially if they respect him. As their paragon you must set an example—follow the same rules that you set for them. If you demand promptness, *be* prompt. If you forbid smoking, *don't smoke*. If you demand neatness and cleanliness, *be* neat and clean. And you must be consistent in your actions.

Your attitude toward the school, the press, and the public will be reflected in the way the team conducts itself on and off the court. Their behavior will mirror their respect for the coaching staff and the coaching philosophy.

The coach must, of course, understand that he cannot please everyone. But as long as he knows that everything he does comes straight from his heart, with the boys' interest always coming first, he can coach with an easy conscience.

Pre-Season Meetings

The boys' indoctrination can best be launched through a preseason meeting. The date of this meeting will depend largely on your conference or league rules. But the quicker you get the boys thinking the right way, the greater will be your opportunity to help them improve themselves.

If you're the type of coach who refuses to become involved with the boys until the first day of practice, you're in the wrong business.

We hold our meeting shortly after school opens in September. We welcome everyone back from their summer vacations and immediately begin to express an interest in their schoolwork. This is our first opportunity to let the boys know that we're interested in what they have done, are doing, and the progress they're making academically.

The Basketball Bible

We then pass out the rules and regulations that they'll be expected to observe during the year. Each boy is given a complete set of mimeographed materials, wrapped in a folder, that we call our "Basketball Bible." The psychological impact is invaluable. The boys are impressed with the fact that their coach took the trouble to have the materials printed, and quickly realize that he must be serious about it.

The Bible reflects our general and specific philosophies and lets the boys know what will be expected of them. They're also given to understand that our rules and regulations are designed primarily to help them, not restrict their freedom.

We make certain to limit the materials to essentials. This tends to lend them more weight and to encourage the boys to take them more seriously. We speak from 15 years of experience, from overhearing veterans warning newcomers that "He really means that." or "He's not a bad guy, but don't break any rules."

Your image and authority will depend on how you handle the violations of your rules and regulations.

Our first meeting also includes a discussion of the materials in the Bible. These include the school rules and regulations, study habits, social behavior, training rules, pre-season practice instructions, regulations for practice sessions, games, bench conduct, and attitude, and an evaluation sheet with which each boy will be expected to assay his progress up to a certain point of the training season.

This seems like a great deal of ground to cover at one meeting. It is, but it's covered only tersely since all of it is always available in each boy's Bible. At this stage of the school year, all we really want to emphasize is the importance of their education. The basketball part of the Bible assumes primary importance once we begin official practice.

It may be fitting at this point to explain our basic rules and our thinking on them. Though our rules are geared to our particular situation at Long Island University, other coaches can adapt many of them to their own situation.

Rules and Regulations for Dormitory Athletes

1. *The athlete must abide by all of the rules* that apply to students living in a dorm.

2. *Rooms are to be kept clean* and available for inspection at all times. Though some boys may hail from fashionable homes and others may be living in a clean place for the first time, all must be sold on the necessity of living in a clean and neat environment. We generally have one of our coaches or trainers drop in every so often just to make certain the boys are practicing the proper health habits.

3. *Curfews.* We observe the same curfews as the regular dorm students until the start of practice. We encourage the boys to get at least eight hours sleep every night. During the season the curfew is 11:00 P.M. from Sunday to Friday and 1:00 A.M. on Saturday. Curfews vary for game nights, with the specific time being set at our special post-game meeting.

4. *Special Requests and Permissions.* The player cannot sleep away from the dormitory. If he wants to go home for some reason, he must get special permission from the head coach. If I won't be available, I'll delegate the authority to my assistant, the athletic director, or someone else familiar with our boys.

5. *Year-'Round Training Rules.* The basic training rules that apply during the training season, such as no smoking, drinking, or gambling, are expected to be observed all year 'round—both on and off the campus.

My feeling is that a boy shouldn't be expected to live right only during the basketball season. What's proper for him then certainly should be proper for him during the entire year. The coach must develop good *permanent* habits, or he's only kidding himself. It's admittedly difficult to break the college boy of poor habits, but the coach must try. The boys must understand that they're representing not only themselves but their institution, coaches, teammates, and schoolmates.

6. *Dress and Appearance.* We expect our boys to be neat and clean at all times. We urge them to be careful of their grooming, and

prod them whenever they tend to become sloppy. A coach must understand that boys differ in background, environment, parental training, and high school training. Once the coach fully understands these differences, he can exercise more patience with the boys who need more help than others.

7. *Attitude.* We continually stress the importance of getting along with all types of people—teachers, teammates, etc. The boys are continually told that they're no different or better than anyone else, nor deserve any special privileges just because they have a special athletic skill.

After enough hammering the boys will begin getting the message. They're also told that we don't want faculty members telling us about a "wise guy" basketball player or about an athlete who refuses to do his work. We mete out punishment according to the nature of the crime, making sure to inform the boy exactly why he's being penalized.

8. *Personal Problems.* Everybody has them, and young people going through their growing stage usually have more than others. They should have someone to turn to. If they believe in you, they'll come to you. Our door is always open. We consider it a privilege to serve as confidante and advisor. The coach who says, "I don't care what's bothering that boy. I'm just interested in how he performs," is breaking every rule of the professional educator. Happily there are few such men in the profession.

9. *Schoolwork* comes first. The boys are told the eligibility rules and given a special mimeographed sheet on "How to develop good study habits." They're informed that all of the baskets in the world will avail them nothing without a good education.

10. *Associations.* We're all judged by the company we keep. I've become famous at Long Island University for my motto that "Garbage attracts garbage." Our boys are instructed to keep good company, and we do all we can to check on them. We're not afraid to tell a boy—in strong language—that he's a fool to associate with anyone we consider undesirable, that all this character has to offer him is trouble. It has reached the point where a boy who is associating with undesirable characters will become self-conscious whenever he sees one of the coaches. We want him to become self-conscious if he's associating with people who are only wasting his time or getting him into scrapes.

11. *Spare Time.* We try to encourage the boys to use the library and to help weaker teammates with their studies. We also direct them to any hobbies they might enjoy. We don't want them "hanging around," wasting time. Some boys have trouble making the adjustment from high school, where they were always told what to do and where to go. When they find all this extra time on their hands, they often waste it.

12. *Set an Example.* We expect the athlete to set an example for the student body—to conduct himself with dignity and to accept praise with humility. As an athlete he has a special opportunity to display leadership. We want him to participate in student affairs, to be a leader and not a follower. We want him to make the students, administrators, and faculty proud to have him in the University.

13. *Proper Conduct.* We let the athletes know that the coaches and faculty will be constantly appraising them on the campus, in the classrooms, in the dining rooms, and all other areas outside of the gymnasium. We want our athletes to be accepted as responsible students who know how to conduct themselves at all times. Whenever an athlete starts ducking certain teachers, you can bet he has been derelict somewhere. We have a great deal of faith in our athletes and we expect them to do a good job academically, socially, and athletically.

14. The rules and regulations must be posted on the bulletin board in every boy's room as constant reminders of the athlete's responsibilities.

Conference Rules Sheet

The next insert in our Basketball Bible consists of the rules of our conference. The boys must know these rules and understand that they're designed for their protection.

Realistically, we cannot list every rule of the NCAA and ECAC. It would swamp the boy with small print and cause him to skip over most of them. We focus on the most important rules, such as, "You will be ineligible if you receive compensation, or accept an award which does not comply with reasonable specifications as to value, type, and source."

Another extremely important rule is the one that makes players ineligible for participating in "outside basketball" either before or after the season. If not properly instructed many of the boys will join outside teams and play all year 'round.

There'll always be boys who break rules and violate faith and trust. The coach should never play ostrich with rule-breakers. He must inform the boys of the rules and then enforce them.

On the high school level, it's wise to both post the conference rules and explain exactly how a boy can lose his eligibility.

Study-Habit Suggestions

The third section of our Bible is entitled "Planning Your Study Habits." It informs the boys that "Your success as a student will hinge in great part upon your study habits. Those of you who developed good habits in high school will have an easier time. Those who haven't will have to work much harder."

The following suggestions are offered to everyone:

Dormitory athletes—study between classes whenever time permits and between 7:00 P.M. and 10:00 P.M. every evening. Lights out at 11:00 P.M. On Saturdays and Sundays put in as much time as is necessary.

Follow this schedule daily. It will enable you to concentrate upon your studies. Always remember that a good study routine will help prepare you for your chosen career and give you an opportunity to play varsity basketball throughout your stay at L.I.U.

A student should develop the following habits:

1. A positive attitude.
2. Study with intent to recall.
3. Understand what you're studying.
4. Take brief notes.
5. Realize that some material is more quickly absorbed than others.
6. Put special stress upon the points emphasized by your teachers.
7. Raise questions as you read.
8. Focus all your attention upon what you're studying.

Training Rules (Year-'Round)

So far the Basketball Bible has stressed rules, regulations, and instructions dealing with academics and social demeanor. The reason for this is simple. We want our boys to understand right at the outset that this is more important for their future welfare than the actual game.

The next section of our Bible consists of our training rules. As previously mentioned these are *year-'round* rules, not just for the basketball season. Most of them constitute commonsense admonitions that require little explanation. I briefly touch upon each, explaining exactly what I expect. (A coach must always remember that every boy is different and may adhere to certain rules in his own fashion.)

1. No smoking, no drinking, no gambling.
2. Be careful of your friendships and associations; stay away from all potential trouble-makers.
3. Eat well, but not excessively, at regular hours.
4. Drink a good deal of water during the day, but not during practice (the reasons for this will be given later on).
5. Report any injury or illness immediately to the coach or assistant.
6. Get plenty of sleep (eight to ten hours).
7. Shower daily.
8. Be careful of your grooming and dress; always give a neat, cleancut appearance.
9. Maintain a friendly and dignified attitude toward teammates, fellow students, teachers, coaches, etc.
10. Schoolwork must always come first.
11. If you have any personal problems, the coach's door is always open.

Remember, your adherence or lack of it to these training standards will show up in the daily practice sessions. To become a good ballplayer, you must be willing to live by these few rules—all of which have been designed for your welfare. All good athletes have denied themselves various pleasures. But it's a small price to pay for athletic excellence and the benefits that come with it.

Some of the qualities it takes to become a good ballplayer:

1. Team spirit and cooperation.
2. Desire for winning and improvement, an eagerness to learn.
3. Pride in yourself, teammates, coach, and school.

4. Confidence in yourself and teammates, developed through hard work, knowledge, skill, and self-discipline.
5. Self-discipline—follow the team rules and set some of your own.
6. Leadership—direct and encourage teammates, take charge without offending anyone.
7. Play tough; let your opponent know he has been in a battle.

Basic Fundamentals

The next section contains a brief résumé of the key fundamentals that every college player must understand and master. (The high school coach should explain these in detail and illustrate them with diagrams.)

- *Passing*

  1. Pass away from the defensive player.
  2. Deliver the ball so that the receiver can quickly shoot, pass, or dribble.
  3. Bounce-pass against a big man; throw over a little man.
  4. Feed the low pivot man from the sides; feed the high post from the middle.
  5. Avoid fancy passing, don't be a showboat. Model yourself after Oscar Robertson—do everything the easy way.

- *Types of Passes to Use*

  1. Chest—aim for the area between the receiver's shoulders and belt line.
  2. Overhead—make the receiver stretch for the ball.
  3. Baseball—used for pitch-outs; avoid wind-up and curves; hit the receiver between the shoulders.
  4. Bounce—deliver the ball at or below the receiver's knees—not above.

We avoid emphasizing such passes as the hook, behind the back, and other fancy stuff. If the boy is an unusually gifted passer or must use a fancy pass out of necessity, we give him such license. But we don't want him making a fancy pass whenever a simple pass can do. We'll always reprimand him for this.

- *Cardinal Rules After Passing*

1. Cut toward the basket, or
2. Screen toward your pass, or
3. Screen away from your pass.

Shooting Fundamentals

Not too many years ago most coaches had every boy shoot the same way, according to a clearcut style delineated by the coach. Today almost every coach allows the boy to use his own style. It makes sense. Our kids begin shooting at a very early age and by the time they reach high school nearly all of them have mastered a distinct style of shooting; and in most cases it's a style that produces results.

The only boy we tamper with is the kid who continually shows a bad percentage or is making some obvious mistake that must be corrected. We do, of course, put in a lot of extra time with the big men. Since they usually have the best shots and do the most shooting, we want them to be as accurate as possible.

As a rule, I'm more interested in (1) having the boy understand what we mean by the good percentage shot, (2) having him shoot that shot as often as possible, and (3) encouraging him to keep taking the good shot regardless of what kind of night he is having.

- *Types of Shots*

1. *Jump*—shoot at the peak of your leap, lining up the shot while you're hanging in the air.

2. *Layup*—expect to get fouled; use the backboard. During practice use the left hand on the left side of the board and the right hand on the right side; during the game use the hand with which you're most sure of scoring the basket.

3. *Set*—either one hand or two. There's nothing wrong with the old two-hand set if a boy has it to go along with the jump shot. The more shots a boy has, the harder he will be to defense. Emphasize aim, concentration, fingertip control, follow through, and follow up of the shot.

4. *Foul*—this must become a mechanical shot and should be practiced every day under varying conditions. Each boy must shoot 50

fouls either before or after practice, and record the results on his own chart. If he cheats, he's only fooling himself. We also shoot fouls during our drills while the boys are running up and down the floor, and during our scrimmage sessions. Generally the boys who drive the most will draw the most fouls. They need the feel of game conditions to derive the most out of their foul-shooting practice.

Shooting is a matter of constant practice. It's not difficult to get boys to shoot. They love it. The problem lies in motivating them to shoot *properly*. This can be done through a series of competitions that will make the practice meaningful. Have enough basketballs for everyone. Every boy wants to become a good shooter and scorer, and it's up to you to find the proper daily motivation.

Dribbling Fundamentals

1. Practice with both the right and left hands; the drills (stop and go, sideway drill, etc.) should be designed with this is mind.

2. *High Dribble*—used for speed whenever you steal the ball and have a long way to go; push the ball way out in front of the body.

3. *Low Dribble*—used for protecting the ball in offensive area and driving toward the basket off screens. Try to keep the ball below knee level.

4. *Protection of Ball*—use the outside hand, keeping the body between the ball and the defender. Try not to cross the ball in front of your body while dribbling.

5. *Fancy Dribbling*—the unusually good dribbler will have a tendency to "sit" on the ball. Everyone should be aware of the basic principle that the fastest way to move the ball up the floor is by passing rather than dribbling. Against the press, the less dribbling in the backcourt the better—unless you have an extraordinary dribbler who can easily beat the sort of pressure being applied.

Defensive Fundamentals

This part of the game cannot be overemphasized. Even on a poor shooting night, a good defense can keep you in the ball game. This is the toughest part of the game. It's seldom reflected in the box score, and there's little glory in it.

The smart coach will use this fact to establish a rapport with the players and the team as a whole. He'll continually praise any boy who makes a defensive contribution, both privately and publicly. The non-scorers who play good defense can thus be made to feel appreciated.

- *Tips for the defensive man:*
  1. Don't cross your legs unless compelled to by the situation.
  2. Don't turn your head.
  3. Keep the outside foot back and the inside hand extended toward the ball-handler's face.
  4. Play in front of a deep pivot man.
  5. Play alongside of a high post.
  6. Overshift on your man if you discover he goes only one way.
  7. Make your man dribble away from his strength.
  8. Stay with your man after he shoots—block him out, count one-two, then go get the ball.
  9. When retreating on defense, don't turn your back to the ball; run sideways if possible.
  10. Always know where the ball is, without losing sight of your own man.
  11. When guarding a man without the ball, overshift toward the ball side and be ready to help your teammate.
  12. Acquire a thorough knowledge of all of your team defenses and positions in case you're called upon to play a variety of positions.
  13. *Special defenses*—such as guarding a man all over the court, regardless of whether or not he has the ball. You'll always be told exactly what's expected of you, and you'll be permitted to break our fundamental rules in order to put pressure on a particular player.
  14. Talking on defense is an absolute must. Players can talk to the opponents if it bothers them, but we're more interested in having our players communicate with each other.
  15. The man who sees a block developing must call it early—loud and clear.
  16. Switches are generally called by the back man, but no matter who calls it the reaction must be reflexive and instantaneous.

Off-Season Practice Suggestions

During the off-season the boys are completely on their own. If they don't participate in other sports, we want them to follow the special instructions included in our Basketball Bible. The hungry, aggressive competitor is always trying to improve himself, and the coach will be able to tell which players have done any work during the off-season.

1. Run, exercise, and work with the weights (as prescribed for you during the season).
2. Do your running out of doors (distance primarily), concentrating on the development of stamina.
3. Volleyball is an excellent activity for teamwork, alertness, and exercise. Play it as often as possible before practice begins.
4. Skip rope every day.
5. Exercise before retiring (push-ups, sit-ups, toe-raises, etc.).
6. Make an appointment with the health service department for your medical examination. Have this exam completed before participating in any practice.
7. Get a good start on your schoolwork so that you don't fall behind once practice begins.

Personal Note

Along with all the rules and regulations, we give each boy a personal note which summarizes the philosophy and objectives of our basketball program, as follows:

I would like to see every candidate achieve success both in basketball and his studies. One is no good if it is achieved at the sacrifice of the other.

The boy who works hard at both is sure to get the most out of college and is most likely to succeed in his future endeavors.

I'm looking for boys with a good attitude, who are interested in living by the rules and being part of a team. Basketball is a team game in which one bad apple can ruin 15 good ones. We're not going to keep any bad apples in the barrel.

You're expected to conduct yourself properly both on and off the court, and on and off the campus. Your actions and your conduct will reflect on every boy on the team, the University, your coach, you, and your parents.

Take advantage of the opportunity given to you, and repay it with loyalty, honesty, and good character. Good luck for the coming season. I hope that through all of our efforts and hard work it will be a winning one.

I will be in touch with you shortly.

Sincerely,

COACH ROY RUBIN

Organizational Directives

The next section of our Basketball Bible embodies certain directives relating directly to our organization for basketball. Each point is covered clearly and fully in order to assure the proper organization for practice.

Every team game requires a great deal of planning and organization, and this must be spelled out in the philosophy and objectives. By acquainting our boys with our aims, we enable them to strive for specific goals.

I believe that the higher the standards, the harder the boys will strive to meet them. We've all seen boys unable to climb a rope, keep trying and trying until they touch the ceiling. In short we're not afraid to set our goals high.

Though our players must strain to reach our goals, they rarely let us down. They become proud of what they're learning and achieving and they soon start boasting about their coach in such ways as: "Boy, he really works us!" or "He asks a lot of us, but he really knows what he's talking about." As these boys mature they arrive at a deeper appreciation of what we attempted to do.

The college player is always talking about his high school coach. If the player achieved any success in high school, he'll usually say, "We did this or that in high school," or "I know all of this stuff; my high school coach was great." I want him to say, "Gee, this is tough. I never knew you had to follow so many rules and learn so much. My high school coach let us do almost anything we wanted."

Varsity and Freshmen Practice Rules

1. *Be on the floor, properly dressed, on or before time—never later.* We generally start practice approximately 15 minutes after the

last class. Since we always stress team effort, we want everyone to wear the same practice equipment and to conform with our other regulations on good grooming and appearance.

2. *Absence or lateness for practice must be explained to the coach.* The player must report to the coach before he can attend the next practice.

3. *Report to the coach or assistant for preliminary practice drills.* We assign each boy to some specific station where he can work on his weakness. We have stations for rope jumping, weight lifting, foul shooting, pivot play, individual defense, moves, and others at which the players may receive special attention.

4. *Around the world with a partner.* The boys pair off, each duo having a ball, then proceed from one basket to another around the gym. Each basket is earmarked for a different skill. One is for tipping drills, one for rebounding, and others for foul shooting, jump shooting, pivot shooting, and outside shooting. Upon completing their competition against each other, the boys can move to the main baskets and concentrate on shooting.

5. *Practice the shots that you'll be shooting in the games.* We ask the boys to practice from the areas consonant with our attacking pattern.

6. *Never sit down at practice.* Every second you waste is time taken from your improvement.

7. *Hustle, hustle, hustle from one drill to another.*

8. *Stop and stand still whenever the whistle blows.* This permits the coach to make immediate corrections. Everyone can learn from each other's errors.

9. *Help teammates.* The coach must develop a feeling of keen but friendly competition. Each player must feel he's expected to beat out a teammate by outplaying him, not by showing him up. The players should be encouraged to help each other, that each of the other players is a teammate, not an enemy.

10. *No water drinking during practice.* We don't want water to become a necessity to the players. This can easily happen if you allow them to drink whenever they choose. Being used to going without water can be a big help at away games, where the water might have a different taste and thus, possibly, cause sickness.

I also forbid players to go to the water cooler during a timeout. A timeout lasts only a minute and is intended for rest and instruction. Yet how many times have you seen a coach talking to himself while his boys are running all over the place looking for a water cooler? This is poor organization and a waste of a timeout.

11. *Learn the drills the way they are taught,* not the way they may have been taught to you in the past.

12. *Don't argue* with teammates, referees, opponents, or fans; and control any tendency you may have for "rabbit ears."

13. *Accept criticism* as constructive, not as an embarrassment. Be happy if the coach continually talks to you or yells at you. It shows he's interested.

14. *Observe proper health habits.* Use clean equipment, clean towels, and don't exchange personal items.

15. *Attitude.* Come to practice to learn and work. As you practice so shall you play. Don't ever let the coach see you dogging it or over-hear you say, "I'm strictly a game player." You must work hard at practice to improve your skills and achieve your goals.

16. *Personal problems.* My door is always open for boys who leave practice confused. I'm always available to explain anything to a player. I realize that all boys learn at a different pace.

To repeat once more: The materials having to do with basketball, such as these practice rules, aren't covered in detail at our pre-season meetings. We wait until the first day of official practice to focus on them. At the beginning of the school year, we're mostly interested in getting the boys readjusted to their studies after the summer hiatus.

We want them to know that the coaching staff and athletic department are continually stressing academics and that no special favors will be given to athletes. A coach who doesn't emphasize the academic phase of school life is merely exploiting his boys. The coach who is continually selling academics will win the boys' respect both as a person and as a leader. It also pays to remember that old players are always returning to the gym to watch the games and visit with the players. If you have been consistent over the years, they will sell your philosophy for you.

Game Rules (Varsity and Freshmen)

1. Prepare all of your game equipment at least a day in advance of the game.

2. For home games, have both your home and away uniforms available.

3. For away games, check with the manager to determine the meeting time, departure, and means of transportation.

4. Be on time, be ready, don't keep everyone waiting for you.

5. The entire team will leave together, travel together, sit together, and return together.

6. You must wear a sport coat, shirt, and tie on every occasion that you're representing the University.

7. No guests, friends, parents, etc., are permitted on team vehicles without special permission from the coach.

8. We expect the varsity to pull for the freshmen and the freshmen to pull for the varsity. Attendance at freshmen games builds camaraderie between the older and younger players.

Game Warmup and Bench Organization

1. *Hustle out* and get a good warmup, just as before practice. Don't do anything different. Use the same layup and shooting drills. And remember, the warmup is for loosening up, not for putting on a show for your friends in the crowd.

2. *Show lots of pepper* and noise during the warmup drills.

3. *Locate the clock and your bench.*

4. *Take assigned seats on the bench.* This prevents scrambling for seats and enables the coach to know exactly where every player is.

5. *Leave vacant the seat* next to the coach. Whenever a player comes out of the game, there's a reason for it, and I want him to know what it is, whether good or bad. He must sit next to me. I don't want him to plump down near the end and begin sulking.

6. *The bench is expected to be "alive,"* with everyone being in the game.

7. *Don't yell at the referee* or get off the bench to fight. Almost every fight on the floor is a flash affair and can be quickly controlled —as long as the benches don't get involved.

8. *Run off and on the court* when going in or coming out of a game. This reflects enthusiasm and creates proper attitudes.

9. *Run off the court to the locker room* at half time and at the end of the game. We don't want anyone standing around taking bows and talking to the crowd.

10. *Everyone must attend a brief meeting at the end of every game.* We don't allow the boys to clear out in ones and twos. We hold a brief meeting, at which we relay any pertinent announcements and check to see if everyone is all right. We also pass on the details about the next day's practice, set the curfew for the night, and offer a congratulatory word if we won or a soothing (or admonitory) note if we lost. Over the years this post-game meeting has become a great tradition and morale booster for my teams. I can't recommend it strongly enough.

11. *Team leaves together.* This completes the coach's responsibility and can be extremely important in areas where there may be hostility attached to the rivalry, though the players are rarely the trouble-makers.

Self-Evaluation Sheet

The last item in our Basketball Bible is a self-evaluation sheet for the players. We ask the boys to evaluate themselves periodically; this gives us a good opportunity to determine what they think of their progress.

We, in turn, use the same sheet to give the athlete our opinion of him. Most of the time the two opinions coincide rather closely. If we find the boy's thinking way out of line, we'll bring him in for some constructive advice.

The evaluation sheet is entitled, "Four Parts to Basketball—At Which Do You Excel?" The four categories are Defense, Dribbling, Passing, and Shooting. We ask the boy to rate himself in each of these categories in the following manner: A—good to excellent, B—fair, and C—poor.

We also ask the boys to answer the following questions:

1. Ability to handle yourself in each of the four fundamentals.
2. Willingness to cooperate with teammates.
3. Interest and ambition.
4. Personality and appearance at practice.
5. Personality and appearance in classes.
6. Dependability.
7. Ability to comprehend and apply.
8. Attitude toward basketball.

9. Leadership ability.
10. Success thus far achieved.
11. What have you learned so far? How much progress have you made?

(*Answer on the back of the sheet*)

Under these questions is a note to the effect that every few weeks I will discuss with each player his weak and strong points.

The Final Word

This concludes the Basketball Bible. There are many more rules and procedures that could be incorporated, but up to the present the foregoing has sufficed for our program.

We know that the mere distribution of mimeographed materials is no guarantee of success. It takes a lot of time, effort, aggravation, courage, and consistency to make all of the players understand what you're attempting to achieve.

You must always practice everything you preach . . . set an example . . . live up to all of the mottoes that you probably have hanging on your locker room walls, such as:

"Don't Let George Do it."

"Don't Quit."

"Practice Makes Perfect."

"There's Only One Endeavor Which You Can Start at the Top, and That's Digging Holes."

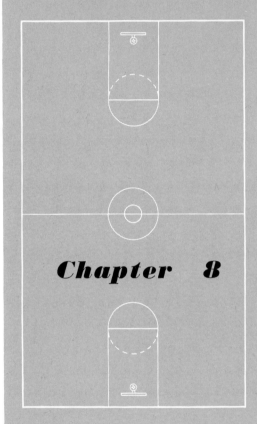

Chapter **8**

CONDITIONING
AND
SPECIAL DRILLS
VERSUS
RESSURE DEFENSES

WHENEVER YOU FACE A TEAM THAT relies heavily on pressure defense, you can count on them being in prime physical condition. To compete with them and challenge their staying power, your boys must be ready to go the full game at top speed. They must be convinced that nobody in the country can outrun, outhustle, or outlast them.

To produce this sort of conditioning, you must do a good selling job—prepare your boys mentally for a lot of hard and often tedious work. Without superlative conditioning, you simply cannot meet the demands of modern-day basketball.

Hundreds of fine drills are available, enabling the coach to be selective. With time of the essence and every phase of the game requiring its own special drills, the wise coach will concentrate on simplicity. The simpler the drill, the less time that's needed for explanations.

As we're concerned here with attacking pressure defenses, we'll focus on the drills that relate directly to our preparation for such defenses.

In our early practices we explain the nature of our routines, how they're related to our system of basketball, and why we'll have to work so hard. All of our conditioning work thus becomes meaningful.

Since drills become boring with constant repetition, we employ a lot of variety and try to install one new drill every day. This not only helps the team enjoy practice, but gives them the feeling that the coach really "knows his stuff" and has gone out of his way to prepare the best possible program for them.

Though there are few new drills—only variations—it isn't difficult for an industrious coach to pick up all the drills he can possibly use. With all the clinics, books, and magazines available to coaches, anyone can develop an interesting and useful assortment of conditioning drills.

In planning our first practice session, we keep conditioning uppermost in mind. Each boy, upon entering the gym, has definite tasks to perform.

Rope Jumping

The boys must first report to the assistant coach for a skip rope. Ropes are inexpensive and there should be enough on hand to accommodate everyone. No boy should have to stand around and wait for a turn at one.

We're not interested in developing fancy boxer routines. If you have any boys who are good enough to get fancy, you can use them to demonstrate. The boys enjoy this. *Make sure that every boy participates.* The theory that only the big uncoordinated man should bother jumping rope no longer holds true. Rope jumping can benefit everyone. It develops timing, rhythm, agility, and leg strength. Constant early-season rope jumping will also help minimize ankle and knee injuries.

Our boys are required to skip rope three minutes every day. By the end of the third week, most of the boys can discontinue it. But those who still show a need for coordination must stay with it. Upon completion of the three-minute stint, each boy is required to engage in a variety of tipping drills.

Tipping Drills

These drills are done by everyone out for the team, regardless of his size, for the same basic reasons as rope jumping. We feel that these drills help develop timing, rhythm, agility, and leg strength.

The tipping drills are done individually at any free basket in the gym. If enough baskets aren't available, we'll have some of the boys work against a wall, tipping the ball against a spot about ten feet up (basket height).

The drills consist of the following:

1. The player tips the ball with his right hand five times, trying to tip it into the basket on his fifth attempt. Each tip must be above the height of the basket. The well-coordinated boy will make each tip with a good even spring, keeping the ball on the same level.

2. After five tips on the right side of the basket, the boy must move to the left side and repeat the drill with his left hand. This generally is more difficult, as most boys are right-handed. The coach can discern the boy's progress in coordination by simply checking his rhythm.

3. The next routine is a two-handed rebound drill, in which the boy tosses the ball against the board at basket level, catches it at the top of his leap, comes down with it, throws it up again, jumps and catches it with two hands again, etc., five times. He must always rebound the ball at the top of his leap, and put the ball into the basket on his final jump.

4. The fourth drill is the same as the third, except that it's done on the opposite side so that the boy learns to rebound both sides of the basket.

5. The boys work together, one on either side of the basket, repeating the first four drills. Instead of tipping to themselves, however,

they must tip across the hoop to their partner without having the ball touch the rim until after the fifth completion. Since this is difficult, the coach should take this opportunity to praise outstanding work and improvement.

The younger and generally the taller the boy, the less coordinated he will be. The coach must not expect too much too soon. As these tipping drills are rather difficult, the boys should be apprised of their purpose—as they should be of almost everything done and taught in practice.

The tipping drills take up no more than three minutes, after which the squad proceeds to the medicine ball passing drills explained in a previous chapter.

Working with Weights

Upon completion of our work on the fundamentals, we proceed to the next body-building drill, which incorporates the use of weights. We use a maximum of only 40 pounds, and work on the weights three days a week, generally Mondays, Wednesdays, and Fridays.

We confine this work to toe raises and squat jumps, as studies have proven that these exercises can increase a boy's jumping ability from two to six inches. In short the purpose of our weight program is developing jumping ability rather than muscle bulk. The light weight (40 pounds) can be handled by even the weaker boys and thus encourages everyone to work hard.

Isometric ropes are available to anyone interested in building strength. But, insofar as strength-building is concerned, the best results have been achieved with the traditional barbells. The boys seem to be more impressed with the weights and work harder at them in the few light drills we give them.

Calisthenics

Next, the entire squad is lined up for a series of calisthenics, with one of our physical education majors serving as leader—a different leader being selected every day. Though we let our P. E. majors give the calisthenics, we expect everyone to learn from them and eventually take a turn as leader.

The boys are informed that these drills will be given for just the first three weeks of practice, unless we feel that *we're* not progressing rapidly enough, Notice the emphasis on *we*. Though a coach should make the decisions, he can, by letting the boys participate in some of them, get them to take a bigger interest in the program.

The coach must, however, determine whether they're being honest or just out to dodge work. He should develop a rapport with his team and make them so hungry to be in good shape that they'll work even harder than he asks them to.

The calisthenic drills should consist of exercises involving every part of the body. We employ the following:

1. Push-ups—for the arms.
2. Sit-ups—for the stomach and waist.
3. Leg Raises—for the stomach.
4. Bend and Stretch—for the back.
5. Toe Raises—for the ankles, calves, and arches.
6. Bicycle—for the legs and hips.

Calisthenics frequently are more important on the high school level, since varsity athletes are excused from the required gym program and thus fail to develop the proper exercising habits. When asked to do calisthenics or other activities in the required program, they'll generally give a less satisfactory performance than the non-athlete.

Reviewing briefly: The order of our drills has been as follows:

1. Rope Jumping (3 minutes).
2. Tipping or Tapping (5 minutes).
3. Medicine Ball (10 minutes).
4. Weight-Training (7 minutes).
5. Calisthenics (5 minutes).

The entire routine has taken only 30 minutes. Though we give it to the boys every day, we make them understand that exercise alone isn't the answer to perfect conditioning. They must eat right and live right as well.

Foul-Shooting Drill

At this stage in our practice session, we give the boys an opportunity to relax with a foul-shooting drill. The players pair off, two to a ball, and must shoot 50 free throws. They're told to step off the line after every shot, just as in a game (where they'll never never take more than two shots at a time).

One boy shoots while the other retrieves. After every five shots they switch assignments. The manager records the totals every day on the players' individual charts.

To make the foul-shooting drills competitive, we have the boys shoot against each other, with the loser having to run as many laps as the points he was beaten by.

The desideratum is 45 out of 50 attempts. The practice charts enable us to determine the better foul shooters after a few days, and we then pair them off against each other.

After reporting their foul shots to the manager, the boys are given a free-shooting period in which they can work on the shots that they'll be taking in the games. This period also gives them a chance to relax, as most of our practice sessions are pretty regulated and the boys need a breather now and then.

Combination Drills

We're now ready for our combination drills. These are lead-ups for our scrimmages later on, and combine conditioning with skills. Each drill is planned in advance and carefully timed so that we won't be spending too much time on one area to the neglect of another. Of course there'll be times when we want to concentrate heavily on an area that requires additional work. But every coach, if not reminded of the time, is prone to apportion his time improperly. Our manager or assistant coach is expected to remind us of the time spent on every drill. Both have a copy of the practice plan for the day.

We demand perfection in this drill period. We except the boys to execute these drills flawlessly within a few days; we accept errors only in the beginning. After that a flagrant violation is penalized with laps around the gym. The running of laps is also part of our conditioning program.

Lay-Up Drill Under Pressure

We start with our regular lay-up drill under pressure, as shown in Fig. 2-1. This is the drill in which the offensive man dribbles to the basket at top speed, while the defensive man, starting from behind, tries to catch up and block the shot or make the dribbler stop and reverse his path. The players then alternate lines. This drill is run on both sides of the court, with the dribbler laying up the ball with the left hand on the left side and with the right hand on the right side.

The drill isn't completed until the ball is retrieved by the defensive player. If the attacker retrieves his missed shot, the two players continue to play one-against-one. This drill (1) puts the dribbler under pressure to shoot properly with a man chasing him from behind, (2) keeps the defender conscious of the need to block out the shooter so that he can't get back a missed shot, and (3) gives both men practice in one-on-one basketball (whenever the shooter does retrieve the rebound).

If the defender does give the dribbler a second shot, he is penalized (after the ensuing play) by having to circle the gym backwards twice —running along the boundary lines just outside the court.

Backwards-Running Drills

We run all of our laps backwards the first three weeks of practice. Our reasoning is that at least 50% of every game is played on defense, where the boys are constantly moving backwards. This is far more difficult than running forwards, and our drills help the boys develop the balance and coordination needed for it.

When running backwards in groups, they automatically make the boy in front of them their opponent. This motivation facilitates their backward circling. The backwards running also puts additional stress on the calf and thigh muscles, thus helping develop the legs. We've had very few problems with leg cramps, and we attribute this in great part to our backwards running.

After explaining why we run our laps backwards, we find our boys accepting it and beginning to believe that it's easy to press all over the court. All-court pressing, they feel, becomes just a matter of running backwards a longer distance.

Every once in a while we'll run our laps in the conventional manner (forwards), and our boys have come to accept this as a reward for
practice excellence.

Since we expect to be pressured anywhere on the court, we set up
our drills on the assumption that the pressure will be full-court.
Hence, all of our drills are run full-court. We want to prepare our
boys to go full-court under pressure for 40 minutes at top speed.

Full-Court Pressure Drills

Our first full-court conditioning drill is done without the use of
a basketball. As shown in Fig. 8-1, we divide the squad into two equal
lines, one on the right side of the basket and the other on the left.

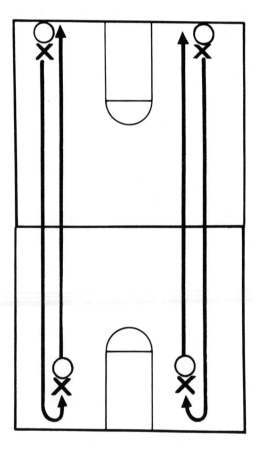

Figure 8-1. Full-Court Press
Without Ball

The first man in the line turns and faces the second; he becomes the defensive player. He places his hands behind his back, locking his thumbs.

At the command (a sharp whistle), the boys start to run from one end of the court to the other. Upon reaching the opposite end, they switch assignments and return.

In our early practices the offensive man isn't expected to elude his guard. The emphasis is on defense—taking a crouched stance and learning to run backwards while staying in front of the attacker all the way.

Though most coaches want their guards to concentrate on some area of the opponent's body, such as the belt-buckle, I have been getting extremely good results with a solider type of positioning. I want my man to square off exactly in front of his opponent's shoulders and to maintain this position at all times, always concentrating on the opponent's shoulders.

Once the boys develop some sort of condition, we begin varying our full-court pressure drill. As shown in FIG. 8-2, we now run the drill over more of the court, rather than in straight lines from end to end.

The players first break to a spot on line with the foul line, then return to their original positions, proceed to mid-court, return, go to the far foul line, return, then go whole court and return. This is an excellent conditioning drill without the use of a ball. Also note that the players switch assignments with each change of course. (The same drill is used for dribbling practice, with the dribbler alternating hands on each dribble.)

After the defensive player learns to run backwards and stay in front of his man, we make him run the same drill with his hands straight up in the air. This helps develop balance and also serves as a habit-former—playing defense with the hands up.

The next conditioning drill is called the "Stop and Go." The players form five lines at the end line. On the whistle they run as fast and as far as they can until the next whistle. This means stop in your tracks. Each succeeding whistle means go, stop, go, etc. This drill helps sharpen the reflexes, makes the boy run at top speed, teaches quick stop-and-go action, and develops alertness.

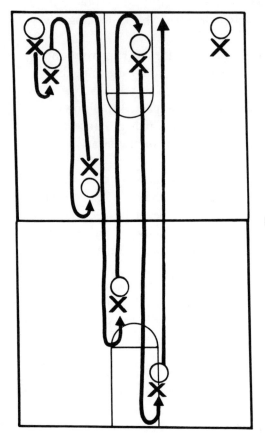

Figure 8-2. Change-of-Course Drill

Group Drill for Quick Changes of Direction

This is an old drill used by many basketball and football coaches early in the conditioning program. All of the players line up across the width of the court, with a leader out in front. He points in a specific direction, and the players immediately shuffle that way. This sort of reaction is helpful in developing reflexes and defensive slides.

Obstacle Races

As shown in Fig. 8-3, the team is divided into three lines, with a balloon dummy placed in the path of each. On the command "go" the boy runs as fast as he can toward the other end of the court, avoiding the dummy in his path. After reaching the other end, he

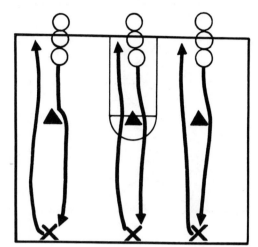

Figure 8-3. Forward-Backward
Obstacle Race

must return backwards. If he touches the dummy, he must do it all over again.

The winning team runs one lap backwards around the gym, the second team takes three laps, and the last place team gets five laps.

Monkey in the Middle

We form a circle in each of the three circles on the court, as shown in FIG. 8-4. One boy becomes the monkey in the middle. The men on the perimeter must keep at least one foot on the circle while passing a medicine ball to each other.

The monkey tries to touch the ball. Whenever he succeeds, he exchanges positions with the thrower. Later on in the season we put two men in the circle and switch to a basketball. This gives us a zone pressure situation—there's little space and two men coming at the passer. To avoid turning into a monkey, the passer must get rid of the ball quickly and accurately.

Dribbling Conditioning Drills

Straight Race: The team is divided into two lines at the end of the court. At the command the boy dribbles down the court with his right hand and returns dribbling with his left hand.

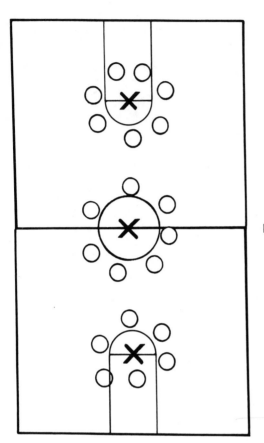

Figure 8-4. Monkey in the Middle

Figure 8-5. Four-Corner Drill

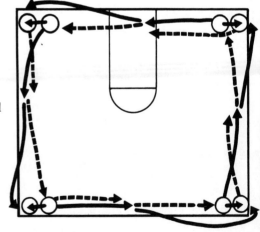

Sideways Dribble, Backwards Dribble: This is the same as above except that the dribble is executed first sideways and then backwards.

Fun Drill: The boys move up and down the court dribbling a ball with each hand. This is excellent for control and coordination, as well as amusing to do and watch.

As a variation of these drills, you can have the boys stop at each court unit (foul line, mid-court, offensive foul line, opposite end line) instead of going full court. The degree of your conditioning should determine the stopping points.

Ball-Handling Conditioning Drills

One of the best that we've used for years is the "Four-Corner Drill." As shown in Fig. 8-5, the team sets up in equal lines at the four corners of the gym. We start with one ball. The first man hands off to the second man and breaks directly toward the second line (counter-clockwise).

The ball man hits him with a baseball pass on the inside of the court. The receiver then throws a chest pass to the first man in the second line, who hands off to the next man and takes off, looking for a baseball pass. This is repeated until everyone has had his turn.

Once the drill takes on some semblance of organization, a second ball is introduced and the drill is started from opposite corners. With further progress a third ball can be introduced and then a fourth, which means that the drill will be launched simultaneously from each corner.

The number of balls used in this drill furnishes an incentive for the players. You want them clamoring for more and striving for records.

Two- or Three-Man Downcourt Fast-Break Drill

This particular drill can be started with two men on the end line. They run parallel to each other, chest-passing a ball back and forth the entire length of the court and back.

The next step is inserting a third line, with the ball being passed from the middle line to either side, back to the middle, then to the opposite side while running at top speed. See Fig. 8-6.

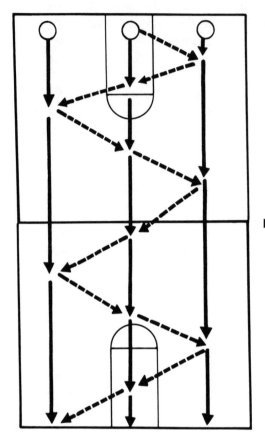

Figure 8-6. Three-Line Fast Break

The twosome or threesome can go up and down the court several times, depending upon how much exercise you wish to give them or to punish them for poor execution.

The drill is excellent for conditioning and ball-handling, and it also incorporates several of our fast-break rules, namely: (1) the middle man should never pass to anyone behind him, and (2) the wing men must get an angle in front of the middle man. If they don't get this angle, we know they're not hustling.

This drill, which started as a two-man affair, then developed into a three-man drill, should progress to a four- and then a five-man drill. Once it becomes a full-team proposition, you can install all of your fast-break tenets.

The progression is very sound and it enables the boys to see their fast-breaking offense taking shape.

Circle Drill

This is another very simple, old but effective ball-handling drill. The squad forms circles around the two foul-line and the mid-court areas. At the whistle the three circles start to run clockwise, passing a ball from player to player. At the next whistle the players turn around and reverse direction.

This drill develops effective ball-handling on the move, and encourages alertness and anticipation (for the next change of direction).

Boxing-Out Drills

In breaking pressure the first thing we must be able to do is get the ball. We therefore concentrate heavily on boxing-out drills. Since we've always lacked the big man, we expect every boy to learn and apply this skill.

Our first boxing-out drill is a simple guard box-out that also incorporates shooting practice. As shown in Fig. 8-7, we form two lines at the top of the circle. The first man becomes the defensive player. He assumes the proper stance, with the foot nearer the baseline back and the inside hand up in the shooter's face.

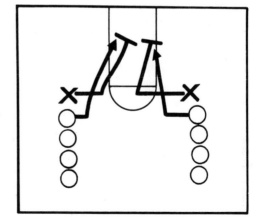

Figure 8-7. Block-Out from Guard Area

The opposite line does the same, with the defensive player slightly overshifted toward the man with the ball. We try to make the situation as realistic as possible, though we let the shooter take an uncontested shot over the guard's extended hand.

As soon as the ball is shot, we make both defensive players exaggerate the correct move. The man guarding the shooter must yell "ball" or any other signal you use to alert teammates to a loose ball.

At the signal the two guards don't immediately turn to locate the ball. They first determine whether their man is going to follow up the shot. They then turn and square off on their man, bending slightly and reaching back to wrap their hands around the opponent's waist. Naturally this is only done in practice to make them remember what we want them to do (box out the opponent). They then count one-two (to themselves) and go get the ball wherever it has fallen.

The guards must retrieve the ball. If their man gets the ball, the guards must stay on defense until they learn to block out and hustle after the loose ball.

This drill is performed in different areas of the offensive court, with forwards playing forwards (FIG. 8-8) and centers playing centers (FIG. 8-9).

At the beginning of the drill, we pair off the players according to position and size. After a few days we expect everyone to be able to fight off anybody. The boys should be reminded that switch situa-

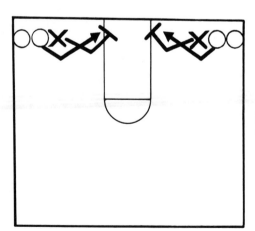

Figure 8-8. Block-Out from Forward Slots

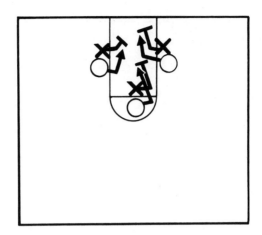

Figure 8-9. Block-Out from
Center Areas

tions frequently occur in which a small man ends up guarding a big
man. The small fellow must know how to turn properly, how to
bend and take up space and force the big man to come down on his
back, if possible.

This drill is done in progression, starting with a two-man drill
and gradually building up to a five-man drill. Fig. 8-10 shows the
full-team block-out drill, and Fig. 8-11 shows the full-team block-out
drill.

What we're trying to do is develop our drills in a manner that will
enable us to handle the press safely and effectively.

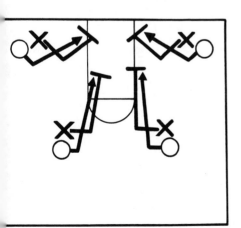

Figure 8-10. Four-Man Block-Out

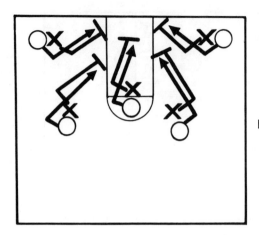

Figure 8-11. Full-Team Block-Out

Fast-Break Drills

After we've mastered the block-out drill with five men, we must decide whether to do any running or just play a control game—be satisfied with getting our percentage of rebounds and then controlling the ball.

We feel that every team should be prepared to fast break. If the opportunity is there, it should be taken. But we don't automatically resort to the fast break—force it even if the situation isn't propitious. Coaches with the personnel can, of course, build their entire offense around the fast break. It certainly can be a powerful weapon, consistently preventing the defense from getting set. So far, however, I haven't been blessed with the personnel to do this.

The prime purpose of our fast-break drills is to beat the defense down the floor and put us in the position of the hunter rather than the hunted. We want to attack rather than merely protect ourselves against the defense.

Three-Line Fast-Break Drill

We start our fast-break work with three lines, as shown in Fig. 8-12. Since this is a progression from our block-out drills, the players line up in their block-out positions. The ball is shot and the men block out and then rebound the ball. The man who retrieves it implements

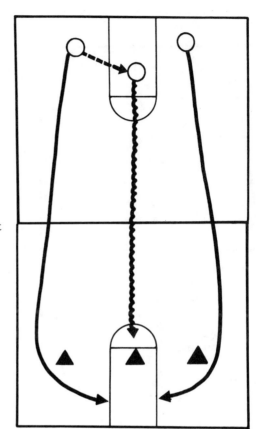

Figure 8-12. Three-Line Fast Break with Advance Man Dribbling

our first teaching tenet—he looks up to see which man is in the better position for the pitchout. He then throws him a baseball pass.

If this man happens to be in front of the other two, the action takes the form of a dribbling fast break. We expect the man to dribble to the center lane as quickly as he can, while the two other players fill in the other two lanes.

The wingmen must overtake the middle man. When the latter reaches the foul line, he must pull up and stop. The wingmen stay as wide as possible, and don't make their cuts to the basket until they're on line with the foul line.

To make sure the players are running in the correct lanes, we set up balloon dummies around which the players must run.

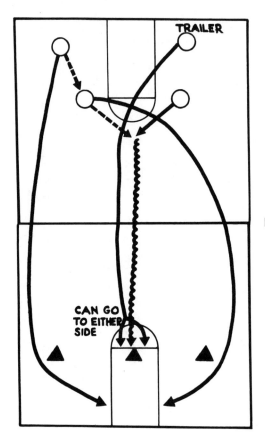

Figure 8-13. Four-Man Fast Break

We then run the same fast-break drill with four men (FIG. 8-13) and, once that's mastered, with five men (FIG. 8-14). Note that we still use the dummies. With four and five men, the fast break has an extra man or two against the three dummies. We want the players to anticipate this advantage and determine where it is.

The next step is the incorporation of defensive players in each of the drills. In using defensive players we always give the offense at least a one-man advantage in order to stimulate game conditions against most pressure defenses.

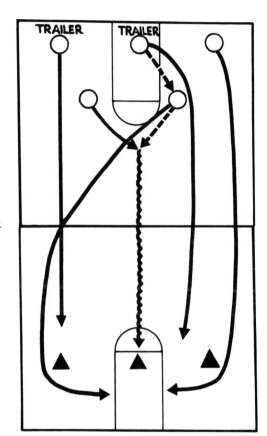

Figure 8-14. Full-Team Break with Double Trailers

Odd-Man Fast-Break Drills

We're now ready for our odd-man drills. We explain that against pressure defenses we're always looking for the 2-on-1, 3-on-1, 3-on-2, 4-on-3, or any other combination that gives us an extra man against the defense. Since this is what we look for in a game, this is what we must practice.

We run the fast-break drill shown in Fig. 8-15 with three men on offense and two defensive men already planted. The feature that

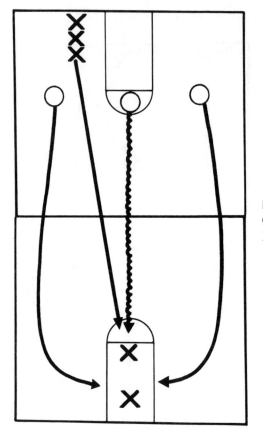

Figure 8-15. Three-vs-Two, with One Defensive Attacker from Behind

makes this drill different from most 3-on-2 drills is that we have a third defensive line that starts a little after the offense. The men in this line chase from behind, as often happens in a game.

The offensive team must get a good shot quickly. But we don't want a rushed shot. If the good shot doesn't materialize, we want the offense to take the ball out and start a three-man maneuver.

This is practiced every day until the boys learn what their best shots are while going at top speed. The objectives of these drills are:

1. To beat the defense down the floor.
2. To get a good shot whenever we have the odd-man advantage.
3. To learn the difference between a good shot and a rushed shot.

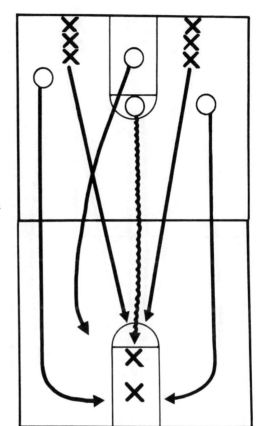

Figure 8-16. Four-vs-Two, with Two Defensive Attackers from Behind

4. To protect the ball by controlling it whenever we cannot get off a good shot.
5. To get practice under game conditions.
6. To practice pattern offense (whenever we can't get the shot).
7. To make defensive players hustle.
8. To practice the shots that we commonly get in a fast-breaking attack.
9. To shoot under pressure.
10. Conditioning.

Since our emphasis here is on attack, we're skipping over the way we play our defensive men in 3-on-2 situations. It should be understood that we drill our men defensively as well. In fact 70% of our

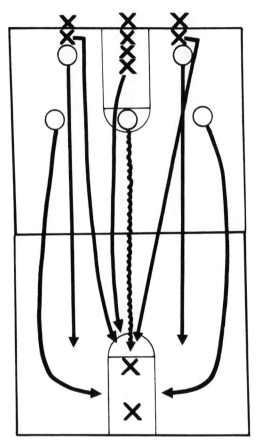

Figure 8-17. Five-vs-Two, with Three Defensive Attackers from Behind

practice is on defense. This is the hardest and the most unnatural part of the game and thus the most difficult for the players to adjust to and learn.

As you can see by FIGS. 8-15 to 17, our boys must be ready to be attacked from behind and the blind side at all times. They are taught to anticipate this in our drills because this is what will happen whenever they come up against a good pressure defense. The drills are designed to give them an awareness of and constant practice on all of the situations that will occur in a game.

Though it's impossible to cover every situation, constant practice will alert and condition the boys to pressure. They must not be

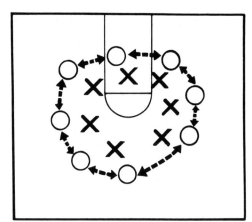

Figure 8-18. Big Monkey in the Middle

allowed to relax during these drills, as they'll never be allowed to relax during the game.

We sometimes shoot fouls during these drills to get the boys accustomed to free throwing under game conditions. We call a minimum of fouls, however, so that the boys will learn to protect both themselves and the ball in those games in which the whistle isn't blown much.

Fun Drills

Fun drills give the boys some competition and relaxation at the same time. But they're still coordinated with our objectives, which is beating pressure defenses.

One of our fun drills is a variation of the previously described "Monkey in the Middle." We call the variation "Big Monkey in the Middle" because we utilize all of the players—half of them in a circle and the other half (the monkeys) inside the circle. (See Fig. 8-18.)

The monkeys can set up anyway they choose, but must keep at least a yard away from the outside men, the passers. The monkeys try to deflect or intercept the ball as it is passed by the perimeter men. As soon as a ball is touched, the teams reverse positions. We try to set a goal of so many passes without an error.

Obstacle Race Drill

Our "Obstacle Race Drill" is shown in FIG. 8-19. We line up the players in three teams and place four or five obstacles in straight lines all the way down the floor. The players must dribble down the floor, weaving around the obstacles—using the right hand when going around the right side of an obstacle and the left hand when going around the left side. Upon reaching the end, they must come back over the course—this time dribbling backwards.

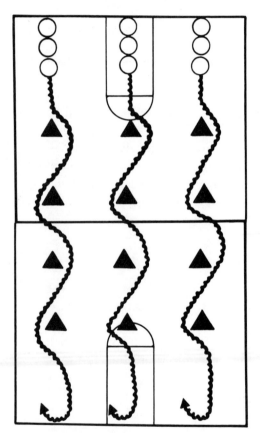

Figure 8-19. Obstacle Race Drill

Two-on-One Jump Shot Drill

This drill is designed to show the difficulty of going through two players and why it shouldn't be attempted. This gives the boys an idea of what we're trying to do against pressure defenses.

As shown in Fig. 8-20, an offensive line is deployed about 25 feet out from the basket, while two defensive lines are placed on either side of the key. The defenders wait for the offensive man to dribble-drive toward the foul line for a jump shot, then close in on him.

Since they have the attacker two-on-one, they're not allowed to foul him while forcing him into a poor shot or a violation.

As you can see all of these drills are not only fun but purposeful.

All coaches have pet drills that they've accumulated over the years. We say use them and get a lot of variety into your practice. But make sure that every drill meets some need of your overall plan.

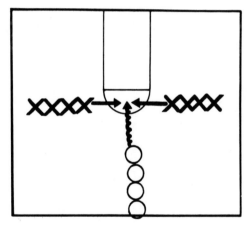

Figure 8-20. Two-on-One Jump Shot Drill

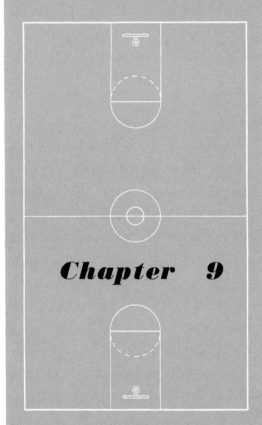

Chapter 9

ORGANIZATION
FOR
PRACTICE
SCRIMMAGES

GIVE ANY GROUP OF YOUNG BASKETBALL players their head and they'll immediately start playing three-man or, if enough players are available, five-man ball. Every boy loves to go full-court and will do so at every opportunity. It meets his need for fun and competition.

You can't fault informal scrimmaging as an off-season device for keeping the boys in shape. But it can be harmful during the season. Where the coach isn't around to supervise the workout, the lack of organization encourages the type of carelessness that produces injuries and bad habits.

Another possible danger lies in the haphazard manner in which the teams are determined. The two best men at one position usually choose the sides. Their choices don't always represent intelligent selectivity. They may choose only friends and deliberately ignore players they dislike. These blatantly biased evaluations are hardly conducive to team harmony and unity. They can cause ill-will and damage a boy psychologically, requiring the coach to put in a lot of extra time repairing wounded psyches.

The scrimmage itself is never completely organized. Each team is usually dominated by one or two men, usually the ball-handlers, and since there is no offensive pattern several of the boys may not touch the ball for minutes at a time. This may cause a boy to react either aggressively, to get his hands on the ball, or non-aggressively—refusing to move unless he has to.

The boys also will play little defense; when they tire they'll hardly ever fall back to the defensive end of the court. With no one around to correct mistakes, the boys will develop many poor habits. In fact about the only benefit of such (unorganized) scrimmage is recreation.

For boys on a varsity or junior varsity team, practice activity should be restricted to organized sessions under the supervision of the head coach or his assistant. If the coaches can't make a practice, the boys should be excused from it.

Intra-Squad Scrimmages

Scrimmaging shouldn't be initiated until the team has rounded into good physical condition and has mastered some of the basic offensive patterns. The scrimmage should always be fully planned, organized, and supervised. The following guiding principles should be observed:

1. The coach should establish his objectives beforehand and then assess the results (after the scrimmage) to see if his goals have been met and what else he must do to achieve them.
2. The boys should be informed in advance of all planned scrimmages.

3. The squad should be divided into teams of equal strength.
4. The scrimmage should, if possible, be played under game conditions.
5. Each squad should be coached (head coach and his assistant).
6. Referees (student managers, former players, etc.) should be used whenever possible.
7. Game rules should prevail.
8. Every boy should get an opportunity to play.
9. Managers should keep score charts and statistics.
10. Benches should be set up as for a regular game.
11. A scorer's table, clock, and scoreboard should be used.
12. The halftime period should be used just as it would in a game.
13. The head coach should correct all errors as soon as they occur.
14. Teams should use definite offensive and defensive patterns.
15. Players shouldn't be switched from team to team.

Let's take a closer look at the reasoning behind these recommendations. By dividing the squad into teams of equal strength, you're giving the substitutes an opportunity to play with the regulars. This gives them the feeling of belonging and promotes squad unity. The fact that you're playing your best against each other also improves the competition, particularly on the high school level where the first team invariably is too strong for the rest of the squad.

By having each team coached, you accustom the players to your brand of bench coaching, game strategy, and discipline. It also makes the practice session more meaningful, and the touch of competition between the assistant and head coaches makes the players work harder and have some fun.

The closer the game condition, the more experience the players will reap. The use of referees will accustom them to play according to the rules and to exercise the proper restraints. Boys who commit their full quota of fouls should be disqualified. Since a team's strategy is usually dictated by changing game conditions, the players can get accustomed to the strategic aspects of the game.

Every boy should be given a chance to play. If he isn't good enough to play, he shouldn't be on the squad. You never know when you might need your No. 9 or No. 11 man. He should be ready whenever you need him, and he should feel that he has a contribution to make to the team.

The managers should learn their game duties during the scrimmages. The coach should indicate exactly what he expects of them and then check on their work. A well-trained managerial staff can relieve the coach of many bothersome duties.

The players should observe the same bench setup as they'll use in a regular game, and should also be required to report to the scorer's table and referee upon entering the scrimmage.

The use of the clock and scoreboard is also extremely important. Since the clock dictates the strategy at any given moment in a game, working either for or against you, the players must learn how to adjust to it. The scrimmage provides an ideal stage for this. With the time element in force, the players can learn how tough it is to control the ball for a long period and how much time it takes to run a certain type of set play. Upon taking the court in an away game, every player should immediately locate the clock and the scoreboard so that he can instantly find it whenever he wants to check the time and the score.

The halftime recess of the scrimmage should be used for correcting mistakes, discussing strategy, making changes in offense and defense, and otherwise getting ready for the second half. The blackboard and other teaching aids should be employed by the coach just as he would during a game.

Both teams should utilize the patterns that they've been practicing during the preceding weeks. The mock game can be used as a testing ground for both pressure defense and the attack against it.

The players shouldn't be switched around freely once the scrimmage begins. If a team loses a strong player on fouls, it must learn to compensate while playing without him.

After the scrimmage, the coach should recapitulate the errors, indicate corrections, and evaluate the strategy. He should make certain to commend outstanding performances, particularly if they were achieved in line with the coach's thinking and instructions.

The coaching staff should then evaluate the performances and begin thinking about how each player can be used to best advantage in the team program. Scrimmage is far more revealing than the daily drills. The veterans invariably look better than the newcomers in the drilling. Being well-versed on the drills, they give a smoother and more skilled appearance. This tends to make the coach believe that they're better athletes than the newcomers.

This isn't necessarily true. The real testing ground, or crucible, is scrimmage. The boys are now under game-like pressure, and several of the boys who looked quite poor in the drills will often show up better than the boys who executed perfectly but who don't really have the competitive fire or poise to play under pressure. The latter type of player seldom will contribute much to the team. Other things being equal or nearly so, the competitor will always make the superior player.

Inter-School Scrimmages

Inter-school scrimmages are valuable adjuncts to the pre-season training program, and coaches who are located in densely schooled areas can consider themselves fortunate. Caution is advisable, however. It's unwise to scrimmage anyone you'll be playing that season. It both blunts the natural rivalry between the schools and gives you too good a look at each other.

A good inter-school scrimmage enables you to get a long, hard look at your players against strange faces. You can thus gain an idea of their aggressiveness and poise—how they respond to pressure and how they react to success and adversity.

You can also observe your patterns in operation against a team that hasn't seen them. It indicates what you need on offense and defense. In short the inter-school scrimmage gives you a good early look at some of your team's weaknesses and strengths. You can then focus on the particular phase of development that your team needs.

The inter-school scrimmage also has a decided value to the individual players. They learn how to maneuver against different types of defenses and defensive players. They also learn a lot more about each other and how to use each other on the court—who becomes nervous and who stays cool under pressure. They begin to understand how the coach will deport himself during the game, and they immediately discover that there's a vast difference between practicing against each other every day and competing against another school.

• *Arranging the Scrimmage*

We try to arrange several scrimmages with schools that are equal or superior to us in ability. There's little value playing a team that you can run over. It won't challenge your boys and it may give them delusions of grandeur.

In arranging these scrimmage games, you must make sure to observe all the covering rules of your league. After deciding upon the date, you should verify certain details with the other coach. You must decide whether the scrimmage will be played under game conditions, the length of the scrimmage, the referees, and whether to permit spectators or make it a closed affair. These details must be settled beforehand. If they're not determined in advance, the scrimmage may be wasted and both schools may go away with ruffled feelings.

Your planning must also include your own team. The boys must be informed on the specifics: the equipment they'll need, where they're going, the place and time to meet, the transportation, and how you expect them to dress and act.

The scrimmage itself can take various forms. You (coaches) may agree to play certain type defenses. You may decide to surprise each other with sudden changes of defense. You may play without the use of a clock or scoreboard. You may only play first team against first team.

It's essential to set a definite time limit before you start. Where the score becomes important to one coach, he can prolong the scrimmage interminably if no time limit has been established.

Varsity-Junior Varsity Scrimmages

Many colleges hold an annual Varsity-Freshman game sometime during the pre-season training period. This traditional game gives the players something to look forward to. The freshmen want to show up the varsity, while the varsity is curious about the caliber of the new crop, particularly if it rosters a hot shot or two.

The game also represents a good basketball showcase for the student body. Every student fan is eager to see both the varsity and the future prospects. Where you have a super star, such as a Wilt Chamberlain or a Lew Alcindor (and who ever gets *that* lucky!), the game may even outdraw many of your regular contests. If nothing else, this sort of game will relieve the monotony of the daily practices.

This sort of game is much tougher to arrange on the high school level, as the junior varsity and freshman teams are usually too young and unskilled to give the varsity much of a battle. A Junior Varsity-Freshman game probably would provide a little more competition. It's up to the coach to decide the type of game that's most feasible and in line with his objectives.

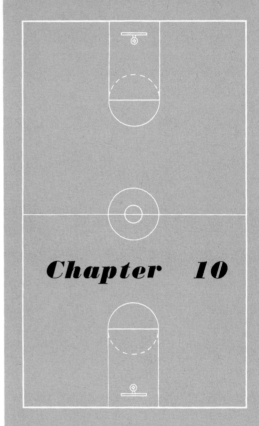

Chapter **10**

SYSTEMATIZED
SCOUTING

SCOUTING HAS ACHIEVED SUCH IMPOR-
tance and respectability that it no
longer is conducted in a spirit of
secrecy and hostility. The atmosphere
between schools is now one of invita-
tion and convenience. Scouting is perfectly ethical and perfectly legal, so
long as you don't try to sneak someone
into a closed practice. It should be
treated as part of the program, and
the coach should neither fear nor
fight it.

Most coaches exchange schedules,
distribute scouting passes to oppo-

nents, reserve special sections for scouts, distribute statistics at the game, feed the scouts, and do everything possible to make them comfortable.

The more complex the game becomes, the more essential is the need for scouting information. This particularly applies to opponents who play pressure defense. If you expect to beat them, you had better learn all you can about their defense.

The general reasons for scouting include:

1. To be able to compete with an opponent on even terms, if they're scouting you.
2. To gain an advantage and thus assure a maximum chance for victory.
3. To be prepared for special defenses.
4. To be prepared for special offenses.
5. To pinpoint the opponent's strengths and weaknesses.
6. To learn an old rival's change of style.
7. To appraise individual players.
8. To familiarize yourself with the opponent's plant (size of floor, lighting, seating, etc.).

Pre-Season Preparation

As soon as you have completed your schedule and receive the schedules of your opponents, you should begin working on your scouting program. The scope of the program will hinge upon the available scouts and the number of times that you want or are able to see an opponent.

It's usually a little easier to scout on the college level, especially if the school has a staff of two or three coaches. In high school, where the coach is often his own trainer, publicity director, and business manager, as well as a classroom teacher, the scouting problem is much more difficult.

That doesn't mean that every college coach has a sinecure. Many of them are in the same boat as the high school mentor, having neither the funds, the time, nor the personnel for a large-scale scouting operation. They often have to rely on friends, professional scouting bureaus, ex-players, and newspaper reports. All of these methods leave something to be desired, as these people don't know your personnel and cannot look at a future opponent as realistically as the coach. An outside agency should be brought in only if the coach cannot do the scouting.

We believe that every opponent should be scouted at least twice. This gives you an opportunity to see a boy against two different teams with two different defenses. A single look often can be misleading, as any boy or team can be having a great night or an off night.

The following points are important for pre-season planning:

1. Obtain the schedule of all opponents.
2. Send a copy of your schedule to all opponents.
3. Arrange scouting assignments for both yourself and your staff.
4. Obtain scouting tickets in advance to avoid running into sellouts.
5. Make your travel arrangements in advance.
6. Plan to arrive at least an hour before game time, especially when traveling to unfamiliar areas or large cities with traffic problems.
7. Prepare all forms in advance.
8. Bring along a partner to chart the shots, preferably someone with a good basketball background who is loyal to you and your school.
9. Prepare the necessary aids for your scouting plans—film, tape recorders, files and records, and all of the proper charts and forms.
10. Obtain as much information in advance as possible from newspapers, brochures, and old reports.
11. Prepare a permanent scouting file on all opponents, to be kept and used from year to year.

The more pre-season planning you do, the better your organization will be. You want to furnish your boys with all the help you can short of actually playing the game for them.

Scouting the Actual Game

After completing your pre-season planning, you should be ready to scout your first game. The only opponent you cannot scout is the one with which you open the season. If you're playing an old rival, you should be able to glean some information from your files. If it's a new opponent, you must attempt to gather information from as many sources as possible, such as newspaper reports, magazine reports, common opponents, friends, ex-players, etc. The only consoling thought about being unable to scout the opponent for your opener is that he cannot scout you either.

The following procedure should be used in scouting a game:

1. Get there at least an hour before game time. This will give you time to get settled, purchase programs, and relax before the teams come onto the floor for their warmups.
2. Check the gym conditions—lighting, size of floor, or any other unusual features of which your team should be made aware.
3. Carefully watch the warmup. Look for the bounce of the ball off the backboard and floor.
4. Appraise the players during the warmup.
5. Watch the key players closely.
6. Notice their shooting habits.
7. Look for poor shooters. This may help in setting up your defense.

Starting the Game

Most teams come into a game with a definite attack and defense. This generally is shown immediately. The scout should, therefore, chart and then begin to plot the offensive pattern against the particular defense that night. This should be done in the following order:

1. Chart the initial tip.
2. Check the scouted team's offensive pattern, as well as their opponent's defense.
3. Check the scouted team's defense, as well as the opposing attack.
4. Be ready to chart all changing defenses and offenses.
5. Indicate at what stage of the game the team changed and why you think they did.
6. After you've become familiar with the team patterns, concentrate on individuals.

7. Chart the individuals in their order of importance to the team—who makes the team go, chief rebounder, chief shooters, etc.
8. Look for special situations—out-of-bounds plays, jumpball plays, etc.
9. Listen to the crowd remarks; you may learn something useful about a particular player.
10. Determine the effect of crowds on the officials. It pays to learn all you can about the officials. They may be working your game in the near future.

You can see by this brief list that the scout will be kept quite busy and thus must make certain to be in a good seat with good vision, so that he can write while he's watching.

First-Half Recapitulation

At the first half-break, the scout should summarize what he has seen and attempt to answer the following questions:

1. Have I learned their offense as yet?
2. What defenses were used in the first half?
3. What were the defensive weaknesses?
4. What were the defensive strengths?
5. What were the offensive weaknesses?
6. What were the offensive strengths?
7. Who were the leading individuals, both offensively and defensively?

The following characteristics help determine the general strength and weaknesses of the team:

- *Offensively (Team)*

1. Do they like to run?
2. Do they like to take their time?
3. Do they drive to the basket?
4. Do they shoot primarily from the outside?
5. Do they have patience?

6. Do they look to score quickly?
7. Do they crash the offensive backboard?
8. Who does the offensive rebounding?
9. What formations do they use to set up?
10. Do they ball-handle well?
11. Do they show poise?

- *Defensively (Team)*

1. Does the team change defenses? If so, under what conditions?
2. Do they have good balance?
3. Do they hustle back?
4. Where and how do they pick up the offensive players?
5. How is the rebounding?
6. Do they block out?
7. Do they switch well when playing man-to-man?
8. Do they press well?
9. Who are the key players?

Upon the completion of the team characteristics, the scout must turn his attention to the individual characteristics of the players, both offensively and defensively. He must look for the following:

- *Offensively (Individual)*

1. Speed of player.
2. Dribbling ability.
3. Shooting ability—types of shots and areas.
4. Use of both hands.
5. Play without the ball—will he play without the ball, or just stand around?
6. Poise.
7. Favorite shots or side of court.
8. Is he a stationary shooter or does he move for his shots?
9. Can he pass?
10. Can he ball-handle?
11. What are his favorite moves?
12. Does he go both ways?
13. Is he a team man or a selfish player?

- *Defensively* (*Individual*)

  1. Speed.
  2. Aggressiveness.
  3. Will he follow the ball or the man?
  4. Does he observe sound fundamentals?
  5. Will he turn his head, give a lot of room, or play too tight?
  6. Does he block out?
  7. Does he go for the fake?
  8. Does he try to steal the ball?
  9. Does he get back on defense quickly?
  10. Does he rebound?
  11. Does he talk?

The scout must also be able to answer these questions at the end of the game. With so many check-points to account for, the scout cannot be expected to find all of the answers in one performance. This is why we feel that a team should be scouted twice. If this isn't possible, you must do the best you can on the single trip. In some high school leagues, where all teams play on the same day and time, it's almost impossible for a coach to do any scouting. He must rely on some other method of espionage.

Post-Game Report

The scout must put all of his information together while it's still fresh in his mind. He shouldn't put it off. He might be scouting again the next night, and if he hasn't finished his work and come to some conclusions and evaluations he may mix his scouting reports.

The shot charts should be carefully evaluated to determine which players took the most shots. You'll almost always find that the key players on most teams take the most shots. The shot chart will also tell you the areas he shot from, but the scout must determine whether he shot from a particular area because he was forced to or because he wanted to. The team's shot total will generally indicate whether they play a running or control game. The scout must be able to evaluate why they took as many or as few shots as they did.

The scout must also be able to give the coach an idea of how their own team can best handle the opposition's offense and defense.

This is why it's preferable for the coach or a trusted assistant who's familiar with their own personnel to scout the opponent personally. An outsider may make valuable suggestions, but being unfamiliar with your personnel he may suggest playing an individual in a way that's beyond the capability of any boy on your squad. You may have to compensate by playing some type of team defense.

The smart coach will vary his defense and offense from game to game. A team that plays a stereotyped game won't be able to change easily when their basic patterns are taken away by an opponent that's done a good scouting job on them. Every team should, hence, have several patterns in order to change their attack whenever necessary.

Reporting to the Squad

The coach can utilize the scouting report in a variety of ways as follows:

1. Blackboard talk—this can be done with a veteran team who understand your thinking and can learn just by listening.
2. Skull sessions—diagramming and discussing the opponents' offense and defense, with the scout pinpointing the strengths and weaknesses of both the team and the individuals.
3. The scouting report can be mimeographed for distribution among the players.
4. The freshman team or several tailend varsity players can be coached on the opponents' offense and defense, and scrimmaged several times against the varsity.

The method of conveying the scouting report to your team will depend on the available time. For example, if you play two nights in a row, it will be quite difficult to practice against the opponents' offense and defense.

I believe the best method is to have your boys run through the other team's offense as many times as possible. At the same time, you must avoid the danger of over-instruction. The slow learners will try to remember so many things that they may forget to play basketball. The amount of instruction will hinge largely on the type of boys you have and the type of game they've been accustomed to playing. Generally, a good defensive team will be more amenable to instruction than the offensive team that concentrates on outscoring their opponents.

Devices Used for Scouting

The modern scout has available an excellent assortment of helpful aids, including such devices as:

1. *Charts.* You must have a supply of charts that will enable you to work quickly and efficiently, as you won't have the time to write down everything. Shot charts and court diagrams are particularly helpful. The latter can be used for charting offense, defense, pattern play, individual play, etc. You can cover almost every phase of the game with these charts.

2. *Films* are invaluable in scouting, but obviously entail considerable expense. However, many teams will be willing to exchange films of recent games.

3. *Diagrams and Forms.* A great many printed forms can be used to facilitate the scout's work. These list all the pertinent questions, and all the scout had to do is fill in the answers. The "Post Game Analysis" form is especially helpful to the young scout. He can actually see what is required of him; he doesn't have to guess or memorize.

Some coaches have forms for individual characteristics, such as players' name, number, weight, height, etc. The scout merely has to fill in the blanks. A form for starters and replacements enables the scout to indicate substitutions—for whom and in what order. Some forms also include diagrams. Every coach should develop his own forms from year to year, making them as simple and complete as possible.

4. *Tape recorders* have become extremely popular in recent years, enabling the coach to keep a running account of the entire game. He can then replay it as many times as he chooses. Many coaches swear by this device. It permits them to keep their eyes on the play at all times, and to express themselves differently at certain stages of the game. For the coach who finds it easier to verbalize than to write,

the recorder obviously is a boon. Its weakness lies in mechanical failure: If the tape isn't handled properly, you'll be out of a scouting report. All in all the tape recorder is an excellent tool. Inexpensive miniature models are now available which put them within reach of the high school.

5. *Files and records* are useful for providing a line on past performances. The records can tell you whether a player is left-handed, what he scored against you, his speed, etc. Since most coaches tend to go with the same offense or defense every year, your file on past games can come in very handy.

6. *Newspapers* will sometimes give you a line on the coming opponent's outstanding players and the type of team game they employ. The scores of their games will indicate whether they're a running team or a controlled one, and the game statistics will enable you to discern the players who are doing most of the shooting.

7. *Brochures,* prepared and distributed by sports information directors, supply helpful information on outstanding prospects as well as the statistics for the previous year. This can give you a line on the returning veterans and the better young prospects.

8. *Newspapers and magazines* also contain information about the teams on your schedule. On the college level there are many national magazines that publish rundowns of the teams throughout the country. They'll name both the stars and the newcomers who are expected to pick up the slack left by graduating seniors and ineligible players. These reviews can put undue pressure on many teams. Most coaches are aware of the fact that the predictions are intended to sell magazines, and so will disregard them. The players, however, believe what they read and may require larger hat sizes for a while. This can be exploited by a smart opposing coach.

Nobody questions the importance of scouting. It often can spell the difference between victory and defeat. It will never spell defeat if your team is properly prepared. If the team you have scouted comes out with a different offense and defense, your boys must be sound enough to adjust. Your team must be well-taught, well-drilled, and well-poised. If they are, the scouting report will help them make a winning team. If they're not, the scouting report won't help.

You must remember that no scouting report will put the ball into the basket or guard an opponent. Neither can the coach. In the final analysis it all comes down to the players and the depth and quality of their preparation.

INDEX

INDEX